Thomas Harwood Pattison

The History of the English Bible

Thomas Harwood Pattison

The History of the English Bible

ISBN/EAN: 9783337172039

Printed in Europe, USA, Canada, Australia, Japan

Cover: Foto ©Lupo / pixelio.de

More available books at **www.hansebooks.com**

Wycliffe Church in 1340.

THE HISTORY

OF THE

ENGLISH BIBLE

BY
T. HARWOOD PATTISON.

Professor of Homiletics and Pastoral Theology in the Rochester Theological Seminary

PHILADELPHIA
AMERICAN BAPTIST PUBLICATION SOCIETY
1420 CHESTNUT STREET
1894

Entered, according to Act of Congress, in the year 1894, by the
AMERICAN BAPTIST PUBLICATION SOCIETY,
In the Office of the Librarian of Congress, at Washington.

TO S. R. P.,

IN ACKNOWLEDGMENT OF A DEBT WHICH
CAN NEVER BE PAID.

1894.

CONTENTS.

		PAGE
	PREFACE,	4
I.	EARLY MANUSCRIPTS,	7
II.	JOHN WYCLIFFE,	19
III.	WILLIAM TYNDALE,	31
IV.	COVERDALE, AND THE GREAT BIBLE,	53
V.	QUEEN ELIZABETH AND THE BISHOPS' BIBLE,	75
VI.	THE AUTHORIZED VERSION,	91
VII.	BETWEEN THE VERSIONS,	109
VIII.	THE ENGLISH OF THE VERSIONS,	129
IX.	THE REVISED VERSION,	145
X.	THE BIBLE IN ENGLISH LITERATURE,	169
XI.	THE BIBLE AND THE NATION,	221
XII.	THE BIBLE IN SPIRITUAL LIFE,	247

PREFACE.

In the following pages I am to tell the story of the English Bible from Anglo-Saxon times to our own day, and to trace some of the influences which it has exercised upon our intellectual, national, and spiritual life.

The story has been told often before, and at much greater length than my space allows of telling it here. This is especially true of our own century. When Christopher Anderson, the minister of a Baptist church in Edinburgh, published his "Annals of the English Bible," in 1845, he broke comparatively new ground; and did so almost by accident; for his purpose was to write a biography of Tyndale, to which the other portions of his work should be supplementary. The field has been occupied since then by a succession of writers, among whom I would mention with especial gratitude Canon Westcott, and Dr. Eadie. But the increasing number of readers of the English Bible will warrant us in telling its familiar and fascinating story over and over again. What Bishop Butler says of the book itself is not less applicable to its history. "It is not incredible that a book which has been so long in the possession of mankind contains many truths as yet undiscovered."

The chapters upon the influence of the English Bible are the natural complement of those which deal with its history. At the present time there is a strong disposition to lay stress upon this kind of evidence as an argument for the divine origin of the book. The Bible finds us in our best and brightest moods, it inspires our noblest literature, it moves us to deeds of purest benevolence and loftiest patriotism. No history of our national, our social, our intellectual, or our spiritual life can be written without a generous recognition of this great influence. We exclaim with Heine, "What a book! Vast and wide as the world, rooted in the abyss of creation, and towering up beyond the blue secrets of heaven. Sunrise and sunset, promise and fulfillment, life and death, the whole drama of humanity, are in this book."

So far as I know these two lines of study—the history and the influence of our English Bible—have not been pursued hitherto in one volume. The extent of the ground covered by the present writer will account for the omission of many details of interest in the history of the English Bible, and of many aspects of interest in its influence.

My own conviction is that back of all questions as to inspiration and revelation—with which indeed the general reader does not very much concern himself—lie the story of the book itself in which there is no room for speculation, and the history of its influence which is one of our national possessions. Whether we think of the liberty which comes to us in action or in thought, the words of Garibaldi hold good: "The best of allies you can procure for us is the Bible; that will bring us the reality of freedom." T. H. P.

Rochester, April 1, 1894.

I.
EARLY MANUSCRIPTS.

Friar Pacificus.—It is growing dark!
Yet one time more,
And then my work for to-day is o'er.
I come again to the name of the Lord!
Ere I that awful name record,
That is spoken so lightly among men,
Let me pause awhile and wash my pen.
     —*The Golden Legend.*

THE HISTORY OF THE ENGLISH BIBLE.

CHAPTER I.

EARLY MANUSCRIPTS.

THE history of the English Bible falls naturally into two periods, the era of manuscript being the first, while the second follows the progress and shares the triumphs of the art of printing. With each of these periods one great name is inseparably connected. Almost a hundred years before William Caxton set up his rude press at the sign of the Red Pale in Westminster, A. D. 1384. John Wycliffe crowned a laborious life by giving to the English people the Bible in their own tongue. He represents the highest achievement of the manuscript period. Almost fifty years after Caxton started his press, William Tyndale, driven from England and forced to do his work by stealth on the Continent of Europe, succeeded in issuing the first printed English New Testa- A. D. 1525. ment. To him belongs the honor of consecrating the new art to what has since proved to be its largest as well as its noblest use.

In the days of Wycliffe, the English tongue had attained a force and beauty which have scarcely been excelled. He is the father of our own best prose. But back of Wycliffe lie at least seven hundred years of the language, and it is possible to find traces in all these centuries of translations from the Scriptures.

It is with this earliest manuscript period that we are interested now. Possibly the uncouth tongue to which Cæsar listened when he landed on the shores of Britain became before long familiar with the truths of Christianity. Gildas, who merits too well the sneer of Gibbon, that he "presumed to exercise the office of historian," affirms that when, during the persecution under the Emperor Diocletian, English Christians went to their death, "all the copies of the Holy Scriptures which could be discovered were burned in the streets." What is certain is that when Alaric took Rome, a century later, Christianity found full employment for all its energies in disciplining the savage hordes that might otherwise have destroyed it ; and as a consequence "the task of the translation of Scripture among the Northern nations was suspended."[1]

A. D. 303.

A. D. 410.

The oldest manuscript in existence is an English

---

[1] Westcott, "A General View of the History of the English Bible," p. 5.

Psalter, partly in prose and partly in verse, preserved in the National Library at Paris. This translation was made by Aldhelm, who died bishop of Sherborne in the year 709. But of course versions of parts of the Bible may have been made earlier than this. The missionaries who found their home among the rugged moors of Northumbria, no doubt gave to the people in the vernacular the truths which they taught them. The ruins of Lindisfarne Abbey on Holy Island, off the northeast coast of England, "the solemn, huge, and dark-red pile," so happily characterized by Sir Walter Scott, recall the name of Bishop Aidan, who there trained laymen as well as priests in reading and learning the Scriptures. Eadfrith, a later bishop of Lindisfarne, is said to have translated most of the books of the Bible. No pleasanter story comes to us from those old times than that of Cædmon, the cowherd of the Abbey of Whitby, the ruins of which still confront the gray North Sea, the poor brother, songless and dispirited, who sees the harp coming toward him at the feast and escapes to the stable, to hear in his dream the voice of his master saying, " Sing, Cædmon ! sing to me ! " and waking finds that with the morning the gift of song has wakened too. From the translations made for him by his better educated brethren, the humble herdsman

[marginal notes: D., A. D. 651. D., A. D. 721.]

versified the histories of the Bible in a tongue more robust than rythmical ; but his harp, as Fra Angelico's pencil, was never suffered to celebrate any other than sacred themes.

A. D. 673-735.
Of all early translators of the Bible, Bede retains most freshly his charm for the student of to-day. His work was done at the monastery of Jarrow, on the river Tyne, where even yet, in strange contrast with forests of chimneys and furnaces, with an atmosphere poisoned by chemical smoke, and with a soil black with cinders, some scanty ruins of his church remain. Bede, known in later times as *the Venerable*, is one of those fascinating characters who never grow old. To the frank simplicity of the child he added the scholar's range of learning, the enthusiasm of a true teacher, and the piety of a saint. More than any other one man he made Northumbria "the literary center of western Europe."[1] Among the translators before the days of printing, he is the only one of whom it can be reasonably conjectured that he went for his authority to the original tongues rather than to the Latin Vulgate. He owned and frequently refers to a Greek Codex of the Acts. How much of the Bible he translated is uncertain, but we know that his last task was on the Gospel of John. For him death had no terrors, and yet he bade his scholars,

---

[1] Green's "History of the English People," Vol. I., p. 64.

who could scarcely study for weeping, learn with what speed they might, for he felt sure that he could not be with them long. His last day was spent in dictating his version of John to his scribe, and in singing, during the intervals of relief from pain, snatches of cheery songs, rude rhymes in his own English tongue. When the evening came, the boy at his bedside said: "There is yet one sentence unwritten, dear master."

"Write it quickly," was Bede's reply.

And a few moments after the scribe told him all was finished: "You speak truth," said his master, "all is finished now."

The last words of the loving evangelist fitly closed the life of one so like-minded. They laid him on the pavement of his church, where he chanted a final doxology, and on its closing words his spirit passed to its rest.

Alfred the Great prefixed to his body of Laws a translation of the Ten Commandments, with portions of the three following chapters of Exodus, and his death interrupted a version of the Psalms on which he was engaged. Patriot as well as scholar, Alfred saw clearly that no book so surely as the Bible would lay the foundations of a native literature, and it was his ambition that all the freeborn men in his kingdom should be able to read the English tongue. Two versions of the Gospels—the Lin-

A. D. 849-901.

disfarne or Cuthbert, and the Rushworth, still remain to us as memorials of the art and devotion of Northern England in the tenth century. The Cuthbert manuscript, once richly illuminated and bright with gold and gems, is preserved in the British Museum.[1] Originally written in Latin, in the seventh century, an interlinear Anglo-Saxon gloss was added to it between the years 946 and 968, by Aldred, a poor priest—*indignissimus et miserrimus*, he pathetically calls himself—of Holy Island.

In the "Rushworth Gospels," while the glosses of Mark, Luke, and John follow closely the Cuthbert book, Matthew is given in an independent translation. This manuscript again is composed of the Latin Gospels written by MacRegol, an Irish scribe, about 820, and an interlinear translation, added eighty or one hundred years later, and of which the authors say: "He that of mine profiteth, pray he for Owun that this book glossed, and Farmen, the priest at Harewood, who has now written the book."[2]

A patriot as true of heart as Alfred himself was Aelfric, abbot of Peterborough, who afterward became archbishop of York, and who "Englished," as he terms it, the greater part of the Pentateuch, Joshua, Judges, Kings, Esther, Job, Judith, and Maccabees. "Englished according

---

[1] "The English Bible," by John Eadie, D. D., pp. 13, 14.
[2] Eadie, p. 15.

to my skill for your example," he says as he presents the book of Judith to Ealdorman Ethelward, "that you may also defend your country by force of arms against the outrage of foreign hosts." Perhaps the militant parts of the Bible were in his mind when he wrote in his homily "On Reading the Scriptures," "Happy is he, then, who reads the Scriptures, if he convert the words into actions."[1]

Aelfric's translation was in circulation in the tenth century. One catches in his resolute words the spirit of defiance with which Dane and Norsemen were met by successive generations of Englishmen. That spirit was invoked in vain before the resolute will and vast ability of William the Conqueror, one of the greatest men of his own, or of any age.

The Norman Conquest affected English scholarship very much as the victories of Alaric, six centuries earlier, affected the scholarship of southern Europe. The work of translating the Scriptures, even if it did not altogether cease, was checked. A new language had to be imposed upon the people. The conflict between the Anglo-Saxon and the Norman-French was not to be settled in a day. Both tongues can be traced in fragments of translation yet extant; and in the end, the language which resulted from the

A. D. 1066.

---
[1] Mombert, "Handbook of The English Version," etc., p. 17.

struggle was to all intents and purposes the language of Wycliffe and Chaucer. Old forms still lingered, but only to stamp him who used them as uncouth and rustic. The day drew near when a translation of the whole Bible of permanent value could be made. That such a translation existed already is extremely improbable, although Sir Thomas More, Foxe the martyrologist, and Archbishop Cranmer claim that it did. "There are, however, two English versions of the Psalter still remaining which were made early in the fourteenth century, together with many abstracts and metrical paraphrases of particular books of the Bible, translations of the Epistles and Gospels used in divine service, paraphrases of gospel lessons, narratives of the passion and resurrection of our Lord, and other means for familiarizing the people with Holy Scripture."[1] The English Bible, even in its imperfect form, had laid hold of the hearts of the nation many years before Wycliffe was born. Preachers made free paraphrases for themselves, and no doubt did then as preachers have done since, founded their discourses upon misconceptions of their texts. But still the people found life in the words of Scripture. There must have been an unauthorized version of large parts of the Bible which to them carried the authority of law. It is remarkable, that while the poet Chaucer frequently quotes

---

[1] Encyclopædia Britannica, "English Bible."

Scripture, he never uses the words of Wycliffe's version, nor does even Wycliffe himself in his discourses.

Naturalists have found a plant in one of the Western States which is so exceedingly sensitive to any interference with its accustomed life that it shows not only uneasiness but even anger when moved from one place to another. It quivers with displeasure and emits a pungent odor, which drives the enemy from its presence. The sensitiveness of our language is scarcely less marked. Preferring older although less satisfactory translations to the noble version of John Wycliffe, the English people furnished an early illustration of that conservatism which has been in all their history an element alike of national weakness and of national strength. The old word was not to be too readily abandoned, nor was the new word to be too readily adopted in the book which was already so dear to their religious experience. We do well to notice this disposition to cling to household words familiar in the ear, because in all the changes through which our English Bible has passed, from Lutterworth to the Jerusalem Chamber, it has been an element with which even the most prudent of our translators have been forced sooner or later to reckon. Kept within bounds, it has warned the scholar not to trifle without good cause with the pure "well of English undefyled"; while, on the other hand, if suffered to thrust the spirit of intelligent criticism from its right place, it has done incalculable harm.

It was while the language of England was being molded and made ready for Chaucer and Wycliffe, that the Bible received the name by which we know it to-day. For a time it seemed as if Jerome's title, "The Divine Library," would win its way to general acceptance; but in the thirteenth century the Greek term "The Book," passing into the vocabulary of the West, became by a slight grammatical misapprehension, no longer plural but singular. "The Books," in popular use was transformed into "The Book"; not one alone but manifold, with an inward rather than an outward unity, true throughout its pages to the personal characteristics of every writer, and to the Divine purpose for the whole.[1]

---

[1] "The Bible in the Church," Brooke Foss Westcott, p. 5.

II.
JOHN WYCLIFFE.

A good man was there of religion,
And was a poorë Parson of a town,
But rich he was of holy thought and work;
He was also a learned man, a clerk.
—*Chaucer.*

John de Wycliffe, D. D.
From Life of Wycliffe, by Robert Vaughn, D. D.
Page 21.

CHAPTER II.

JOHN WYCLIFFE.

THE latter half of the fourteenth century is memorable in the history of popular freedom. The monopolies of the favored classes were challenged by the people as never before. Italy saw the brief but splendid resistance to the nobles led by Rienzi, "consul of orphans, widows, and the poor." In France, the peasants sublimed to power by despair, and stimulated alike by hunger and oppression rose against their lords, firing their castles and murdering their wives and children. The passionate appeal against brutal tyranny which culminated in England in the revolt of Wat Tyler was smouldering long years before. The country was suffering from famine and plague, and her best blood was drained by her wars. How long she could endure, and whether indeed the world itself was not near its end, were questions on many lips. The time, so many thought, must be at hand when the Judge would come, if he were not already at the gate—

> To terminate the evil,
> To diadem the right.

A. D. 1320-1384. To this England John Wycliffe addressed himself as the consciousness of his powers and obligations grew upon him. Although born in 1320, near Richmond in Yorkshire, and not far from the village which still bears his name, he matured slowly. Nothing distinguishes him more than the self-possession with which he moves among the troublous elements that he was mastering and controlling for God and "merrie England." From his peaceful mastership of Balliol College, Oxford, he "leaned out his soul and listened." Everywhere he saw civil commotion and ecclesiastical change. The papacy rent by internal disputes was ill prepared for resisting the growing spirit of revolt in England, whose people would no more brook a foreign usurpation of their consciences than they would brook a foreign invasion of their soil. In 1356, he began the work which has made him famous, by translating the Apocalypse, perhaps attracted to that book, as was Savonarola in the next century, by the apparent fulfillment of its prophecies in his own land and age. This was followed by the Gospels with a commentary; and by 1380 he had translated the whole New Testament, including a revision of the Apocalypse. Wycliffe was now sixty years old, but it seemed as though he had lived many lives since his public course began. As a statesman, he had supported his sovereign in his resistance to the pope, and had incurred popular disfavor for a time by his attachment to John of Gaunt, the most powerful noble of his day. As a reformer, he had stimulated the revolt of the people against the oppression of their superiors, and was charged with giving John Ball, the mad priest of Kent, his most powerful arguments when he inquired in his homely way:

> When Adam delved and Eve span,
> Who was then the gentleman?

Since 1361 he had been a parish minister, incessant in his labors for the welfare of his charge. Almost a quarter of a century he had given to the work of translating, and throughout a period of like duration he had been evangelizing England, and by means of the itinerant toils of his "poor preachers" spreading his doctrines broadcast over the land. The Old Testament was added to the New in 1384. Apparently it was begun by Wycliffe's friend and disciple, Nicholas de Hereford, who proceeded as far as Baruch 3 : 20, when he was forced to lay down his pen at the beginning of the verse by a summons to appear before a synod of preaching friars, and at their instigation was excommunicated.[1] He escaped, and returned from Rome to England, but not A.D. 1382. in time to see his old master. Probably Wycliffe himself finished the work begun by Nicholas de

---

[1] Eadie, Vol. I., p. 64. Stoughton, p. 33.

Hereford. However that may have been, the translation of the Bible completed in 1384 was substantially the work of John Wycliffe. It was finished only just in time, for on the 28th of December he was stricken with paralysis while hearing service in his own church of Lutterworth, and died as the new year was coming in.

Wycliffe's version was made from the Latin Vulgate, and from the impure text current in his time. Within a few years of his death his followers became so conscious of its defects, that one of the foremost of them, John Purvey, a fellow-sufferer with Nicholas de Hereford, prepared a complete revision which was issued in 1388. "A simple creature," he says of himself, "hath translated the Bible out of Latin into English." His quaint account of his method suggests some of the soundest principles controlling any translation: First, this "simple creature" had much travail with divers fellows and helpers to gather many old Bibles, and other doctors and common glosses, and to make one common Bible some deal true; and then to study it of the new, the text with the gloss and other doctors as he might get, and specially Lyra on the Old Testament, that helped him full much in this work; the third time, to counsel with old grammarians and old divines of hard words, senses, how they might best be understood and translated; the fourth time,

A.D. 1388.

to translate as clearly as he could to the sense, and to have many good fellows and cunning at the correcting of the translation.[1] According to his facilities, his method was that of the more learned divines who, centuries later, took up his work in the Jerusalem Chamber.

How untrustworthy the manuscripts of the Vulgate then were is shown by Purvey's statement that "the common Latin Bibles have more need to be corrected, as many as I have seen in my life, than hath the Latin Bible late translated."[2]

We are attracted to Purvey by the simplicity of his nature, and by the scholarly modesty that led him to "pray for charity and for the common profit of Christian souls, that if any wise man find any default of the truth of translation, let him set in the true sentence." The "simple creature" lived an unsettled life, was imprisoned for his opinions, and in 1400 recanted at St. Paul's Cross. Of the one hundred and fifty copies of his version known to us, all appear to have been written before 1430, by which time Purvey himself was dead. But there must have been many later manuscripts, for although proscribed in convocation by Archbishop Arundel in 1408, the book was circulated widely, and more than any other version was the Bible of the English people, until the printing press gave the place of honor to the trans-

---

[1] Westcott, p. 16.   [2] Ibid., p. 18.

lation of William Tyndale in the next century. The work of Wycliffe and of Purvey was done at a time when the thought of the nation, as well as its speech, was in a state of transition. Translating as they did, not from the original, but from the Vulgate, there are traces in their versions of ecclesiastical dominance and of theological error. The word *clergy*, which stout James Melville the Presbyterian said smelled of papistry, although used by the congregation of believers, frequently occurs, so does *sacrament* where later versions use *mystery* (1 Tim. 3 : 9); and *penance* for *repentance;* and *priests* for *elders* (Titus 1 : 5). But there is often music in the sentences which once heard cannot soon be forgotten, as when the man cúred of blindness at the pool of Siloam, says: "*I wente, and waischid, and sai.*" There is a tenderness lacking in later versions, in *Persida, moost dere worthe womman* (Romans 16 : 12). The play on language is very effective in such a verse as *Alle thingis ben nedeful to me, but not alle thingis ben spedeful* (1 Cor. 6 : 12); and there is sound teaching in making Paul say (1 Cor. 14 : 38): *If ony man unknoweth, he schal be unknowen*, where in our later version we read, *If any man be ignorant, let him be ignorant*. The noble description of Moses' old age in our version is perhaps more dignified, but it is certainly not more graphic than Wycliffe's : *Moises was of an hun-*

drid and twentie yeer whanne he diede; his ize dasewide not, nether his teeth weren stirid.[1]

That Wycliffe's Bible should be inferior to our authorized version is not to be wondered at. Even had he been one only among a large and learned company, and favored with royal patronage as well as with scholarly leisure, this would have been natural. We must consider under what disadvantages he worked. How rapidly at that time the language was changing is seen at once by contrasting his earliest version, of 1380, with that of Purvey of 1388. But the impulse sprang from peaceful Lutterworth to which we are indebted for our Bible to-day. Priestly proscriptions were powerless to arrest the circulation of the book, which found most favor in Purvey's revision. Some of the copies still extant, to judge from their size, were evidently the friends and companions of their owners in the home and on the road; but others were counted fit to be the gifts of princes.[2] Foxe is no doubt right in saying that within thirty-six years of its first publication by Wycliffe, the sweetness of God's word had been tasted by great multitudes, and that to read and hear it well-disposed hearts sat up all night. To obtain the book in England "some gave five marks [about two hundred dollars] some more, some less for a book;

---

[1] "The Bibles of England," by Andrew Edgar, D D., p. 8, et seq.
[2] Westcott, p. 24.

some gave a load of hay for a few chapters of St. James or of St. Paul."

Wycliffe's work was all done between the years 1356 and 1384, and probably no Englishman in so short a time has made so deep and lasting an impression on his land and age. He stands at the source and fountain head of the Protestant Reformation, and draws his faith direct from the pages which he translates. If he anticipates Luther at the desk, he anticipates Wesley in the field, and sends out his itinerants preaching, bare of foot and clad in unbleached russet, to evangelize the land. While his wide and generous scholarship taught him to reverence human reason, his temperament and training taught him equally to reverence authority. The first may have made him a Protestant, but the second kept him in humble submission to the Scriptures. His preachers bore with them on their journeys the conviction that their master inculcated nothing which he had not first experienced himself. With a frame as frail as Calvin's, he possessed not a little of the same restless energy, indomitable will, and impetuous spirit. At the same time he had popular gifts, geniality, humor, audacity, a love of the right, a hatred of all falsehoods and fraud, a wealth of invective and of persuasion, which bespoke his English blood. Our space has allowed us only to glance at the mighty influence which John Wycliffe exerted not only upon his own country, but also upon the whole continent of Europe. Heroic John Huss gave utterance to the feelings of thousands of devout souls when he said, in refusing to condemn Wycliffe: "I am content that my soul should be where his soul is." He came to an age which many different influences had combined to make ready for his message. Speaking at the Wycliffe Commemoration, in 1881, Dr. Stoughton said: "There was an intellectual activity—there was spiritual life throughout the period. The nadir was in the tenth century; the fourteenth saw the dawn of modern civilization. Society then appears on the move; feudalism was in decay; cities were rejoicing in newly sealed charters. Parliaments in England were asserting their rights; commerce had left its cradle full of energy and life. The springtime of poetry had opened, and Chaucer had gathered the crocuses and snowdrops. God every now and then sends some strong man into the world to do much needed work. The hour calls for the man, and the man comes to meet the hour. The Divine hand that strikes the bell creates the representative fitted to obey the summons. God struck the hour for the Reformation in the sixteenth century, and Luther appeared. A hundred and fifty years earlier, and the bell rung for a reformer before the Reformation. Behold John Wycliffe in answer to that signal!"

In his passion for the Scriptures as containing the words and will of God, he rose above all national distinctions, and from the higher plane of citizenship with the whole world, he dared look forward through the troubled times in which he lived and utter those noble words, which await even yet their full accomplishment: "I am assured that the truth of the gospel may indeed for a time be cast down in particular places, and may for a while abide in silence; but extinguished it never can be. For the Truth itself has said: *Heaven and earth shall pass away, but my word shall never pass away.*"

III.

WILLIAM TYNDALE.

Which he may read that binds the sheaf,
  Or builds the house, or digs the grave ;
  And those wild eyes that watch the wave
In roarings round the coral reef.
—Tennyson.

WILLIAM TYNDALE.
Page 33.

CHAPTER III.

WILLIAM TYNDALE.

OUR English Bible in its printed form was born in exile. The country which, more than any other, was to be distinguished in after years for its zeal in printing and circulating the Scriptures was late in entering the lists. The laboring sounds of Caxton's press had been heard for more than half a century before an edition of the New Testament in the vernacular was printed in England. She was nourishing her faith on manuscript copies of the Wycliffe versions long after the time when Bibles were printed in French, German, Dutch, Italian, and other continental languages.

In the year 1524, a scholarly Englishman, in the early prime of his powers, came to the busy German city of Hamburg, which was already famous as a stronghold of Protestantism.
His name was William Tyndale. A.D.1484-1536.
He was born in 1484, in some quiet little village in Gloucestershire, in the west of England, and it is likely that he had flowing in his veins the German blood which has done so much for the honor of both the Old World and the New. He was "brought up from a child," says Foxe, "in the University of

Oxford, and then went to Cambridge." From the first he was singularly addicted to the study of the Scriptures. At the manor house of Little Sodbury, still standing in his native county, he acted as tutor in the family of Sir John Walsh. Here his enthusiasm for the Bible often brought him into trouble in the dining hall, where he loved to challenge the priests sitting around the table to make good their doctrines from Scripture. The outspoken young scholar caused many an uneasy hour to the lady of the house, who would remind him that learned doctors, worth hundreds of pounds, held views the very opposite of his; and "were it reason, think you, that we should believe you before them?" But Tyndale was even then possessed by the ambition to give to England a Bible which not only wealthy ecclesiastics, but poor peasants also might read. "If God spares my life," said he to one of those priests, "ere many years I will cause the boy who driveth the plough to know more of the Scriptures than you do." At Cambridge he had listened to the sentiment of which this was an echo as it fell from the lips of the famous Erasmus. "I wish," the great Greek scholar had said, alluding to the Gospels and Epistles, "that the husbandman may sing them at his plough, that the weaver may warble them at his shuttle, that the traveler may with their narration beguile the weariness of the way."

A. D. 1520.

Tyndale was no dreamer or fanatic. In giving his life to the fulfillment of his project, he had done so under the conviction that "it was impossible to establish the lay people in any truth, except the Scriptures were plainly laid before their eyes in their mother tongue. . . This thing only moved me to translate the New Testament."[1]

No doubt Lady Walsh was relieved when her tutor took his departure for London. He had heard Tunstall, bishop of England, praised for his learning by Erasmus. In those days the bishop's palace was often the home of poor young scholars waiting for the flood-tide of a better fortune. But Tunstall had no room for Tyndale. It happened, however, that an alderman of the city, Humphrey Monmouth, heard him preach a few times, and was so pleased with his doctrine that, on Tyndale's entreaty, he took him into his house. Monmouth was already a Protestant. It is of him that Latimer, in one of his sermons, tells the pleasant story that, meeting a poor neighbor of his, who lost no opportunity to abuse him for his opposition to Rome, he seized him by the hand and spoke so tenderly to him that the heart of his enemy melted, and falling on his knees asked his forgiveness. Monmouth engaged Tyndale to pray for the souls of his father and mother—"and all Christian souls"—for ten pounds sterling, and in such

---

[1] Westcott, p. 33.

duties, and in hard study day and night, half a year passed. What Gloucestershire had failed to yield him, however, London also refused; and in his own words, the simple-minded, unworldly scholar "understood at the last not only that there was no room in my lord of London's palace to translate the New Testament, but also that there was no place to do it in all England."[1]

A. D. 1524.
So it came about that in the year 1524, Tyndale exchanged the hospitality of the London merchant for what he pathetically calls, "Mine exile out of mine natural country, and bitter absence from my friends." He left London and carried his precious manuscripts to Hamburg.

During the time that he spent here he seems to have published separately the Gospels of Matthew and Mark. In the year 1525 we find him at Cologne, where he was engaged in printing the translation of the entire New Testament. But the difficulties which had beset him in his native land, and which very likely may have driven him from Hamburg, followed him still. His project came to the ears of a deacon of the Church of the Blessed Virgin at Frankfort, one Cochlaeus, whose enmity to the Reformation was roused to the highest pitch by hearing that there were two Englishmen at Cologne about whom the

A. D. 1525.

---
[1] "Our English Bible," John Stoughton, D. D., p. 76.

printers in their less sober moments would boast that before very long, whatever king or cardinal might say, they would make all England Lutheran. Cochlaeus himself describes how far the printing had proceeded : "Calling certain printers into his lodging, after they were heated with wine, one of them in more privat discours, discovered to him (that is, to Cochlaeus himself) the secret by which all England was to be drawn over to the side of Luther—namely, that three thousand copies of the Lutheran New Testament, translated into the English language, were in the press, and already were advanced as far as the letter *K, in ordine quaternionem.*" Cochlaeus adds that the expense of this undertaking was met by English merchants, who were to receive the books and secretly distribute them "throughout all England." The two Englishmen thus betrayed by the babbling printers were Tyndale and an amanuensis, Roye or Joye. The city authorities promptly stopped the printing; and Cochlaeus wrote warning letters to the king of England, Cardinal Wolsey, and Bishop Fisher, so that they might "prevent the importation of the pernicious merchandise."[1] Persecuted in one city, Tyndale was still able to flee to another. Hastily gathering up the sheets already printed of his "pernicious merchandise,"

---

[1] "The Annals of the English Bible," Christopher Anderson, 1845, Vol. I., p. 60.

he took ship on the Rhine, and following Lutheranism to its headquarters, reached Worms, where four years earlier the great Reformer had triumphantly defended his doctrines before Charles V., and where now the new art of printing was being carried to great perfection. A scholarly German traveler in 1526 notes in his journal that at a dinner table where he was entertained, one of the guests told him that an Englishman living with two of his countrymen at Worms, had translated the New Testament, and that six thousand copies had been printed, and that for all the king opposed it, the English were so eager for the gospel as to affirm that they would buy a New Testament, even if they had to give a hundred thousand pieces of money for it." [1]

Resuming at Worms the work interrupted at Cologne, Tyndale determined to issue two editions of the New Testament. The printing of the first, a quarto, had been begun by Guentel before Tyndale's flight. The second, an octavo, was executed entirely at Worms by P. Schœffer, the son of one of the first great triumvirate of printers. This edition was the first to be issued. D'Aubigne probably surmises rightly when he says: "As Tyndale's enemies would have marked the edition—the quarto begun at Cologne—some few sheets of it having fallen into their hands,

A. D. 1525.

---

[1] Westcott, p. 41.

he took steps to mislead the inquisitors, and began a new edition." This is borne out by what Tyndale himself says in a letter to the reader at the end of his octavo : "Count it as a thing not having his full shape, but, as it were, born afore his time, even as a thing begun rather than finished."[1]

Of this little octavo volume, which has been called "the most interesting book in the language," the Baptist College at Bristol, England, possesses the only perfect copy known to be in existence. Although it has been admirably reproduced in *fac simile*, yet to see the original itself, guarded as one guards a priceless jewel, it is worth while to make a special pilgrimage to the old city on the Avon. The historian of the college tells its story : "The precious volume, worth much more than its weight in gold, was originally in the Harleian collection. It was obtained for the Earl of Oxford by one of the many agents whom he employed in hunting for old and rare books. The earl had long wished for such a treasure, and was so pleased when he found himself in actual possession of it, that he bestowed upon the fortunate finder an annuity of twenty pounds. It is stated that Osborne the bookseller, purchased the Harleian library for less than the earl had spent on the bind-

---

[1] " History of the Reformation of the Sixteenth Century," J. H. Merle D'Aubigne, D. D. Ed. Religious Tract Soc., London, Vol. V., chap. 8–10.

ings, and that to insure a speedy sale, he catalogued all the books at a remarkably low figure. Not recognizing the value of this particular book, he priced it at fifteen shillings. It passed into the hands of the antiquary, J. Ames, and at his death, into the hands of a Mr. White, who gave fourteen guineas for it."[1] Mr. White sold it to his friend, Dr. Gifford, a Baptist minister of much repute in his day, for twenty guineas, and Dr. Gifford placed it in the college library.

Bearing no translator's name, the two editions stole into England in the spring of 1526. Lee, afterward archbishop of York, was traveling on the continent at the time, and hearing of the "pernicious merchandise" on its way across the German Ocean, wrote to King Henry VIII. to warn him. "I need not to advertise your grace what infection may ensue hereby if it be not withstanded. All our forefathers, governors of the Church of England, have with all diligence forbid and eschewed publication of English Bibles."

The merchants were importing copies, agents all over the southeast of England were selling them, the people were eager to buy. Sir Thomas More attacked Tyndale for the Protestantism which cropped out in his translations. Tunstall, bishop

---

[1] "Faithful Men: Memorials of Bristol Baptist College," S. A., Swaine, pp. 7-12.

[2] Westcott, pp. 40, 41.

of London, assured the crowds gathered about the preaching place at Paul's Cross, that he alone had found two hundred errors in it. He and the archbishop of Canterbury, Warham, ordered that all copies should at once be given up. Thomas Garret, a curate in London, was tracked by Cardinal Wolsey from the metropolis to Oxford where he had gone to sell copies of the book "to such as he knew to be lovers of the gospel." Casting off his hood and gown, and disguised by a friend who has left us the graphic picture, "in a sleeved coat of mine of fine cloth in grain which my mother had given me," Garret fled. His friend, Dalabor, shutting his chamber door, went into his study, and with his Testament in his hand kneeled down and committed to God his brother "and the tender and lately born little flock in Oxford. This done I laid aside my book safe." All in vain, however. Both Garret and Dalabor were apprehended and with others who later again proved firm in the faith did penance in procession. The book was flung on the fire. The same ceremony with another set of performers was enacted soon after outside St. Paul's Cathedral, London. Wolsey was present, sitting clothed in purple on a great platform, surrounded by abbots, friars, and bishops. Fisher, bishop of Rochester, fulminated from a new pulpit against Luther and his heresy, and great baskets full of New Testaments were burned. "Rochester and his holy brethren," said Tyndale, when the news reached him, "have burnt Christ's Testament; an evident sign verily that they would have burnt Christ himself also if they had had him."

It seems that these copies of the New Testament were mostly bought up at Antwerp, where Tyndale was now living. Hall, the old chronicler, is our authority for the story that Packington, an agent of the bishops who were bent on destroying the book,—"a gracious and blessed deed," said Nix, bishop of Norwich,—came to Tyndale at Antwerp and purchased the Testaments from him direct. "Forward went the bargain," he says; "the bishops had the books, Packington had the thanks, and Tyndale had the money." To sell them this translator would be nothing loth, as he was already anxious to bring out a new and revised edition of his work. What is certain is that the bishops did buy up all the books that they could find, and that their scheme failed in its purpose. Nix who was paid heavily to have the "pernicious merchandise" destroyed, wrote in 1527 to the archbishop that something more must be done. It was reported by many that even the king himself "wolde that they shulde have the arroneous boks"; and "marchants, and such that had ther abyding not ferre from the see" were greatly infected; and from the college at Cambridge which sent the most priests into his diocese not one had come into Norfolk lately "but saverith of the frying pan, tho' he speke never so holely." [1]

Meanwhile the work of printing went forward. Tyndale's New Testament was reprinted without his leave three times before 1528, and in 1534 by his former friend and ally, George Joye, with whom there was henceforth a very bitter feud. "One brought me a copy" (of Joye's edition) says Tyndale, "and showed me so many places in such wise altered that I was astonied, and wondered not a little what fury had driven him to make such a change, and to call it a 'diligent correction.'" Joye, not to be beaten, published what he called "an apology made, by George Joye to satisfy if it may be William Tyndale; to purge and defend himself against so many slanderous lies figured upon him in Tyndale's uncharitable and unsober epistle."

In 1530, Tyndale, turning his attention to the Old Testament, published his English Pentateuch. In this he probably had the assistance of stauncher friends than Joye, and also used largely Purvey's manuscript version. The book of Jonah appeared in 1534, which closed his labors on the English Bible, with the exception of a revision of Genesis, and the revised New Testament which he sent out in the same year. A.D.1534. This has been well called "altogether Tyndale's noblest

---

[1] Strype's "Cranmer," quoted by Westcott, p. 53.

monument."[1] A merchant adventurer of Antwerp, who had suffered for selling Tyndale's books, appealed to Anne Boleyn, now queen of Henry VIII., and as much interested in the Reformation as her shallow and guilty nature allowed her to be; and in gratitude for her favors to his friend, Tyndale struck off for her private use a copy of his crowning work on vellum, beautifully illuminated. Her name, in faded red letters, may still be deciphered on the gilded edges of the book. Before two years were over she had been beheaded in the Tower of London, and Tyndale had been strangled in the Belgian Castle of Vilvoorden. He was lodging at the house of Poyntz, an English merchant, when he was betrayed by a fellow-countryman named Phillips, to whom he had lent money, and with whom he at the moment of his capture was going out to dine, counting him "human, handsomely learned, and very conformable." Poyntz returning home, learned from the officers who had apprehended Tyndale all that had happened, and how he had been carried off to Vilvoorden, eighteen miles away, and imprisoned. Thirteen years the brave translator worked in exile; and the last sixteen months he lay in the dungeon craving in words which recall Paul's, "a warmer cap, being afflicted with a perpetual catarrh, a warmer coat also, for that which I have

---

[1] Westcott, p. 185.

is very thin, and also a candle in the evening, for it is wearisome to sit alone in the dark. But above all, I entreat and beseech that the *procureur* may kindly permit me to have my Hebrew Bible, Hebrew grammar, and Hebrew dictionary, that I may spend my time with that study.[1] It was in vain that faithful Poyntz petitioned King Henry VIII. to interpose, assuring His Majesty that he had no truer-hearted subject. Tyndale was in the clutches of his life-long enemies, and for him there was now only one pathway of escape. On Friday, the sixth of October, they brought him from the cell where he had spent so many cold and dreary hours, and bound him to the stake. Before the executioner strangled him, Tyndale cried with a fervent zeal and a loud voice, "Lord, open the king of England's eyes!" After he was dead his body was burned on the spot. At that very time, and no doubt known to Tyndale, the first volume of Holy Scripture printed in England, an edition of his own revised New Testament, was passing through the press. It was printed by John Godfrey, and closing with the words, "God save the King and all his well-willers," was itself the best answer to the martyr's dying prayer. A.D. 1536.

Tyndale was emphatically a man of one idea. To put the Bible into the English tongue and make it a

---

[1] Demaus' "William Tyndale, a Biography," p. 475–6.

household word in his native land was the ambition of his life. He was willing to be an exile himself if only by being so the Scriptures might make their home there. He was not like Wycliffe, a man of affairs, a statesman, an organizer. Better than any other of the great Englishmen who have been translators of the Bible, Tyndale represents the scholar, pure and simple. He had the scholar's indiffference to comfort and disregard of little courtesies of life. His host, Humphrey Monmouth, says of him : "He studied most part of the day and of the night at his book ; and he would eat but sodden meat by his good will, nor drink but small single beer. I never saw him wear linen about him in the space he was with me." Thomas Poyntz, his friend at Antwerp, tells us how Phillips, on the morning when he betrayed him, with a baseness worthy of Judas Iscariot, desired Tyndale to lend him forty shillings, "for," said he, "I lost my purse this morning coming over at the passage between this and Mechlin." "So," adds Poyntz, "Master Tyndale took him forty shillings, the which was easy to be had of him if he had it ; for in the wily subtilties of this world he was simple and unexpert."[1] In his devotion to the absorbing purpose of his life Tyndale no doubt may have been rude and abrupt in speech when he spoke at all, and we have seen

---

[1] Demaus' "Tyndale," p. 422.

how he could flame up when provoked by those who would rob him of his scholar's honors, and saddle upon him the burden of their own incapacity. His bitterest foe could scarcely draw a less flattering portrait of him than he drew with his own pencil when he pictured himself as "evil favored in this world and without grace in the sight of men, speechless and rude, dull and slow witted."[1]

But the translation of Tyndale marks a distinct advance in the history of the English Bible, not only or chiefly because it had the advantage of the printing press, but because of its own excellencies. With the possible exception of Bede, Tyndale first among English translators turned for his authority to two original languages. Before he left Cambridge, Erasmus, his master and model, had published the Greek Testament, with a new Latin version.[2] He has been charged with drawing his inspiration from Luther, but some years before Luther's Bible appeared, Tyndale's mind was full of the purpose of translating the New Testament, and between his work and that of the German Reformer there are only such points of resemblance as are natural in the work of men so like-minded as were they. It was to the Greek text of Erasmus and to his Latin

A. D. 1516.

---

[1] J. R. Dore, "Old Bible," p. 18.
[2] Westcott, pp. 32, 179.

version that Tyndale turned when he set himself to his task. The young scholar who came up to London to push his fortunes with Bishop Tunstall on the strength of a translation which he had made from Socrates, would appreciate the man who, of all others, gave color to the statement that in that age of quickened intellectual life "Greece had risen from the grave with the New Testament in her hand." The title-page of Tyndale's revised New Testament runs thus: *The New Testament, diligently corrected and compared with the Greek, by William Tyndale, and finished in the year of our Lord God, 1534, in the month of November.* What he understands by correction and comparison he explains in his "Epistle to the Reader," from which a few sentences may be quoted: "Here hast thou, most dear reader, the New Testament or Covenant made with us of God in Christ's blood, which I have looked over now again at the last, with all diligence, and compared it unto the Greek, and have weeded out of it many faults, which lack of help at the beginning or oversight did sow therein." There is a touch of humor in what follows: "If any mind find fault, either with the translation or aught beside (which is easier for many to do than so well to have translated it themselves of their own pregnant wits at the beginning without an ensample), to the same it shall be lawful to translate it themselves, and to put what they lust thereto. If I shall perceive, either by myself or by the information of others, that aught be escaped me, or might more plainly be translated, I will shortly after cause it to be mended."[1] Probably he had the piratical incursions of Joye in his mind when he wrote this, for in a further address "yet once again to the Christian reader," he says: "Wherefore I beseech George Joye, yea, and all others too, for to translate the Scriptures for themselves, whether out of Greek, Latin, or Hebrew. Or, if they will needs, . . . let them take my translations and labours, and change, and alter, and correct, and corrupt at their pleasure, and call it their own translations and put their own names, and not to play bo-peep after George Joye's manner." Tyndale did well to be angry, for Joye's alterations were such as of his own will he himself would never have made, "though the whole world," as he says, "should be given me for my labour."[2]

With Hebrew, Tyndale was not familiar in his early life. He was leaving his native land forever when the chair of Hebrew was revived at the University of Cambridge. Four years later, however, when maintaining the duty of the translator to turn to the original languages for his authority, he says: "The Greek tongue agreeth

---
[1] Demaus' "Tyndale," p. 392.
[2] Westcott, p. 69.

more with the English than the Latin, and the properties of the Hebrew tongue agree a thousand times more with the English than the Latin."[1] It is probable that he learned his Hebrew from Jewish scholars at some of the German cities where he lived. We remember how, from his prison in Vilvoorden Castle, he sent for his Hebrew grammar and dictionary. This suggests that he was studying to the very last, and aspiring to merit the character which had been given him ten years before: "An Englishman who was so complete a master of seven languages, Hebrew, Greek, Latin, Italian, Spanish, English, and French, that you would fancy that whichever one he spoke in was his mother tongue."

The disputes between Tyndale and Joye add pungency to the history of the quarrels of authors. Our sympathy is enlisted on the side of the guileless student who saw his own familiar friend and scholar arrayed in his robes, and bringing discredit on their rightful owner. But for one forward step in the annals of our Bible we seem to be indebted to Joye. He pleaded for the book to be published without note or comment. In a vigorous defense of his course, he says: "As for me, in good faith, I had as lief put the truth in the text as in the margent; and except the gloss expand the text, or where the text is plain enough, I had as lief

---
[1] Westcott, p. 174.

leave such frivole glosses clean out. I would the Scriptures were so purely and plainly translated that it needed neither note, gloss, nor scholia, so that the reader might once swim without a cork." The hint was not thrown away upon one who had declared years before that "to give the people the bare text of Scriptures, he would offer his body to suffer what pain or torture, yea, what death His Grace (Henry VIII.) would, so that this be obtained."[1] A prisoner himself, and only to be set free by the executioner, Tyndale's last act was to give the Bible liberty, and to trust it to defend itself. The edition of 1535, in which for the first time headings were prefixed to the chapters in the Gospels and the Acts, was happier than any of its predecessors, in being issued without marginal notes. Joye was right. The reader of the Bible could be safely trusted to swim without corks. But an immense advance was made when the book was put into the hands of the people in their own language, and left to its own simple, unaided strength. They could tell now for themselves what authority their preachers had for their loose paraphrases and ingenious perversions of the Scripture. The revised New Testament, with which William Tyndale crowned his life of single-hearted devotion, was a plea for the right of private judgment as well as for the authority of the Script-

---

[1] Demaus, p. 410.

ures. It was the most eloquent proof of the translator's faith in Luther's declaration that "it is always better to see with one's own eyes than with those of other people."

IV.
THE GREAT BIBLE.

Now I begin to taste of Holy Scriptures; now, honour be to God, I am set to the most sweet smell of holy letters. . . . Nothing in the world I desire but books as concerning my learning: *they* once had, I do not doubt but Almighty God shall perform that in me which he of his most plentiful favour and grace hath begun.—*Miles Coverdale.*

MILES COVERDALE.
Page 55.

CHAPTER IV.

COVERDALE, AND THE GREAT BIBLE.

TYNDALE was martyred, but the work so dear to his heart went on. In his prison at Vilvoorden, the news may have reached him that what he aimed at was actually accomplished. On the fourth of October, 1535, a year before his death, the first complete Bible printed in the English language was published. Advancing no claim to such thorough scholarship as distinguished the work of Tyndale, this translation was confessedly made from the German and Latin, by King Henry's "humble subject and daylye oratour, Myles Coverdale."[1] It is his story that we are now to tell.

Born under the shadow of the fine old monastery of Coverham, A. D. 1488-1569. in Yorkshire, and bearing a name given to the whole district and still to be read on headstones in the village churchyard, Miles Coverdale was yet young when he was sent to complete his studies at the Augustinian monastery in Cambridge. Here, if not earlier, he would naturally receive a powerful impulse toward the Protestant

---
[1] Dore, "Old Bibles," p. 88.

doctrines, as well as toward the new learning which Erasmus had quickened in the university. Dr. Robert Barnes, who was at the head of the monastery, was earnest in circulating Tyndale's New Testament, likening the Latin version to "a cymbal tinkling and brass sounding." For inveighing against the luxury of Cardinal Wolsey, and for having the obnoxious books in his possession, Barnes was persecuted in 1526, and before the terrible vision of the stake abjured and bore his fagot among the penitents in the Bible burning at St. Paul's. Fourteen years later he played the man courageously and was martyred with his friend Garrett, two days after the execution of Thomas Cromwell, the powerful statesman, who with all his faults of arrogant ambition and timeserving, did more than any other public man to advance the Protestant Reformation in England. Coverdale was from the beginning a reformer. "He was active," says Dore, "in searching out those who had not in obedience to King Henry VIII.'s order defaced the name of St. Thomas a Beckett in their office books; so carefully was this done that the owner of a prymer in my possession, to be quite safe, scribbled over the name of St. Thomas the apostle, as well as St. Thomas of Canterbury." From the beginning, also, Coverdale was sustained in the work which he did by the patronage of others. If Barnes influenced him in his Protestant convictions, those who were far more powerful than the head of the Augustinian house aided him in his work as a translator of the Bible. Cromwell was his friend at a time when the friendship of the great minister meant everything. Cranmer, raised to be archbishop of Canterbury, if he did not directly approve Coverdale's labors, was an ardent champion of the English Bible. His master, Henry VIII., was just then fascinated with "his dearest first wife and most virtuous princess, Queen Anne," and it is in these words that Coverdale refers to his patroness in the dedication of his Bible. How soon that fascination died away is pathetically illustrated by the fact that within a year the dedication bore the name of Queen Jane, who was married to the fickle king in 1536.

Seven years earlier than this, Coverdale appears to have left England for the Continent, and there for some time his work was carried on. Possibly he met Tyndale in 1529 at Hamburg, and helped him on the Pentateuch; but this is uncertain. We know that already his mind was full of his great enterprise, and his quick impressionable nature was fired with zeal for its accomplishment. "Nothing in the world," he writes to Cromwell, "I desire but books as concerning my learning: *they* once had, I do not doubt but Almighty God shall perform that in me which he of his plentiful favour and grace hath begun."[1] A much nobler man than Cromwell, Sir Thomas More, had introduced Coverdale to the minister, and it is probable that both of them urged upon him the speedy completion of his work. By 1534, he tells Cromwell that his manuscript is ready for the press. The printing was finished in October of the following year.

The same mystery which veils so much of the early Bible work hangs about Coverdale's first Bible. It is even uncertain where it was printed. At Frankfort, Zurich, Antwerp—which? A recent discovery has proved conclusively that Jacob Van Meteren, of Antwerp, was at this time employed in producing a translation of the Bible, and that for this purpose he employed "a certain learned scholar named Miles Coverdale."[2] This makes it most likely that our first English Bible was printed in the same city in which Tyndale had been betrayed. In order to conform with an Act of Parliament prohibiting the introduction of bound books into England, Meteren sent the sheets to Nicholson of Southwark, by whom they were made up and published. Nicholson seems to have removed Coverdale's original title-page, which set forth that the book was "faithfully and truly translated out of Dutch (German) and Latin into English"; and to have substituted another declaring

---

[1] Westcott, p. 71.   [2] Stoughton, p. 124.

COVERDALE, AND THE GREAT BIBLE. 59

only that it was "faithfully translated into Engglish." He also added a florid dedication to the king, and the book was further embellished by a map which, as a work of fiction, almost equals the dedication. The title-page is exceedingly elaborate, and seems intended to set forth the common origin of both Testaments. The creation of man, Moses on Sinai, the public reading of the law, John the Baptist preaching in the wilderness, Jesus sending forth his disciples, Peter addressing the multitude on the day of Pentecost, are the Bible scenes represented; while due justice is done to the king by a picture showing him engaged in giving the book to his lords, spiritual and temporal.

"*Biblia:* The Bible, that is the Holy Scriptures of the Old and New Testament," so the title runs. The ecclesiastical term comes first, the vernacular, so dear to our ears, follows. The Apocrypha is included in the translation; the Epistle to the Hebrews is placed between the Third Epistle of John and the Epistle of James, which is itself followed by Jude and the Revelation. A summary of its contents precedes each book. There are no headings to the chapters; the division into verses is not indicated, and, following the later example of Tyndale, there are no explanatory notes. "A true concordance in the margent," adds much to the value of the book,

A. D. 1535.

and later editions contained "many necessary annotacyons after the chapters, declarynge sondry harde places conteyned in the texte."

We have spoken of Coverdale as possessed of an impressionable nature. His work was evidently done at the instigation of others. More and Cranmer were his patrons in England. Meteren employed him at Antwerp. He performed his task "at the cost and charges of others." To help him in his translations he turned, he says, to Latin and German interpreters, "whom because of their singular gifts and special diligence in the Bible I have been the more glad to follow for the most part." [1]

The influence of Tyndale is very evident in the Pentateuch and the New Testament. In other parts he followed the Vulgate, but he was especially indebted to Luther's Bible, three volumes of which were printed in 1524, and the remaining ten, completing the edition, in 1532.[2]

It was probably through no fault of his that Coverdale lacked the robust independence of Tyndale, but still he had to take the consequences. The royal favor for which he set his sails did not come. Nicholson's courtly dedication to the king failed of its objects. No license for its circulation was granted. Cranmer, for some reason, instead of adopting the new translation prepared to have another made; for his convocation in 1534 had

---

[1] Dore, p. 91.   [2] Dore, p. 90.

censured all books of suspected doctrine in the vulgar tongue printed on the continent, and Coverdale no less than Tyndale would be included in this condemnation. Neither royal nor ecclesiastical patronage rewarded the man whose natural disposition it was to trust in them both.

Still there was progress. The book was A.D. 1536. not positively suppressed. The leaders in the church had become anxious, and themselves petitioned that a new translation might be ordered by the sovereign whose servants they were. Cromwell himself presided at a council of bishops and learned men, which must have shown the great minister what strides the Reformation was making among the dignitaries of the church. When Stokesley, bishop of London, sneered at the word of God which every cobbler was reading in his mother tongue, Cromwell and many others gathered around the board did not conceal their merriment at "his old rusty sophistries"; and Fox, bishop of Hereford, made bold to say, in a speech which rose to true eloquence: "The lay people do now know the Holy Scriptures better than many of us. . . . Truth is the daughter of time, and time is the mother of truth ; and whatsoever is besieged of truth cannot long continue."[1] The disgrace and death of Anne Boleyn could no more stay the march of the good work than can the slain on the battlefield arrest

---

[1] Westcott, p. 84.

the rising of the sun. The first edition of Coverdale's Bible was soon exhausted, and others followed, "set forth with the king's most gracious license." For the edition of 1537, Nicholas, bishop of Salisbury, prescribed "a prayer to be used by one reading the Bible." In the same year another composite Bible was ready for publication, made up largely from the work of Tyndale and Coverdale. Once more, but happily for the last time, we have to trace underground the secret history of a Bible the authorship of which is even now uncertain.

A hundred years ago, the name of John Rogers was a household word in New England, and the rude woodcut of his martyrdom was almost the only work of art permitted in a country where art was never much favored. Rogers was one of Tyndale's friends, and chaplain to an English congregation in Antwerp.[1] A Cambridge man, a good general scholar and especially able as a linguist, his intimacy with Tyndale both strengthened his love for the reformed faith and quickened in him a zeal for Bible translation. It was natural that Rogers should be Tyndale's literary executor. A version of the books from Joshua to 2 Chronicles, inclusive, came in this way into Rogers' hands. Upon this he proceeded to put together a composite Bible, made up of Tyndale's translations of the

---
[1] Stoughton, p. 144.

Old Testament as far as it went, with the remainder, including *the Apocrypha*, from Coverdale; while for the New Testament he used the revised edition of Tyndale. Rogers was related by marriage to Jacob Van Meteren, and it is quite likely that the enterprising printer of Coverdale's Bible printed this one also. Two London citizens, R. Grafton and E. Whitchurch, met the expense of the work, which was printed and finished "to the honor and praise of God in the year of our Lord God MDXXXVII."[1] The title-page reads, "The Bible which is all the Holy Scriptures: in whych are contayned the Olde and Newe Testaments truly and purely translated into English by Thomas Matthew." Now who was Thomas Matthew? His name occurs at full length at the close of the dedication, but an exhortation to the study of the Scriptures which follows bears the initials "J. R." Foxe, the martyrologist, is our authority for believing that Rogers and Matthew were one and the same person. In the sentence pronounced on Rogers before his death he is called "John Rogers, alias Matthew," and in the Council Register of Mary's Reign it is written, "John Rogers, alias Matthew is ordered to keep his house at Paul's." The Bible was currently known as Rogers', and if Matthew had a separate personality of his own it is strange that nothing further is known about him.

---

[1] Stoughton, p. 138.

The dedication to the sovereign and his queen, Jane, is effusively loyal, and concludes with a prayer in which multitudes of true English hearts would join, that a son and heir might be granted to them who might "prosperously and fortunately reign and follow the godly steps of his father."

Both Cranmer and Cromwell were interested in the appearance of this Bible. The archbishop prays the minister, in a letter dated August 4, 1537, to show the book to the king, and to obtain a license for its sale, until "we bishops shall set forth a better translation, which I think will not be till a day after doomsday." Within a week, Cranmer was able to tell him that the book, more pleasant to him than the gift of a thousand pounds, had been seen by the king, and leave to buy and sell it freely granted. This was a triumph of diplomacy, for the notes and comments distributed through Matthew's Bible are openly Protestant, and the works of Tyndale, to which the compilers had been so much indebted, had been more than once condemned by the king and his council. Grafton, who had advanced so much money for the printing of the Bible, suggested that a royal command should oblige every curate in the realm to purchase one of them, and every abbey six. "They of the papistical sort," he thought should be compelled to have them. All others, it may be presumed, would need no royal mandate. Certainly the book was eagerly welcomed. Grafton was forced to appeal to Cromwell for protection against certain piratical Germans, who were preparing to republish it for "covetousness"; and but that another and far nobler enterprise was now filling the great statesman's mind, no doubt Matthew's Bible would have been even better known to history than it is. As it was, a London lawyer, Richard Taverner, prepared a Bible of his own, which he issued in two editions in 1539, and which was undoubtedly based upon that of Matthew. It was printed in London by Byddell and Bartlett, at the Sign of the Sun, and prefaced by a manly dedication to the king. Taverner makes no claim to be more than a reviser of previous work, and as he was very much of a pedant—loving to cite the law, in court in Greek, vain of his accomplishments, and preaching, layman although he was, before the young king, Edward VI., in a damask gown, velvet bonnet, and gold chain, we may fairly conclude that he does not make too modest an estimate of his share in this good work. It was this same Richard Taverner who provoked Thomas Fuller by holding forth before the students in St. Mary's, Oxford, in his high sheriff's gold chain and sword, and beginning his discourse thus: "I have brought you some fine biscuits, baked in the oven of charity, and carefully conserved for the chickens of the church, the sparrows of the Spirit, and the sweet swallows of salvation." Fuller had reason for complaining that "preaching now ran very low," if this is a fair specimen of the pulpit oratory of the period.[1] The conceit of it is not more manifest than is its bad taste.

The time was now ripe for a Bible not only approved by the king, but actually issued under his authority. It was to this that Cromwell directed his energies in 1538. Coverdale was to undertake the work. Regnault, of Paris, was to print it with a splendor to which the English presses were not equal. In the early autumn, Cromwell received the welcome news that within five months the Bible would be ready. The inquisitor-general of France, however, appeared on the scene when the text was almost finished, and peremptorily forbade its further progress. Coverdale and Grafton, the generous London citizen who was with him, escaped to England. They were fortunate enough to carry off presses, types, workmen, and even four great dry vats full of condemned sheets, which had been sold to a tradesman as waste paper. Not by any means for the first time, the spirit of intolerance did the cause of liberty a good turn. England now possessed on her own shores men and material equal to carry through a worthy edition of the book in the

---

[1] Stoughton, p. 148.

mother tongue. By April, 1539, *The Great Bible*, as it came to be called, A.D. 1539. translated "by divers excellent men," was completed. If no royal dedication was prefixed to this book, the loss was amply compensated by a magnificent title-page, which Holbein, the court painter, is said to have designed, and in which the king figures giving the Bible to Cranmer and Cromwell, who distribute it among the ecclesiastics and laymen, while below, a crowd, admirably depicted, listens eagerly to a preacher who addresses them from a pulpit bearing the inscription : *Vivat Rex.* The Protestant Church of England was from the first subservient to the State, and Henry was not likely to let this be forgotten.[1] Much to Coverdale's regret, no comments were permitted to be printed with this great Bible, which owed so much to him, although he offered to submit them first of all to Bishop Bonner for his approval. The book, which lives in our literature in the Episcopal Psalter, remains the noblest monument to Cromwell's zeal. When he fell from power, in 1540, it survived his disgrace. Tunstall, the very same bishop who, although a scholar of repute himself, had refused to give the scholar's chamber to Tyndale, and who had afterward preached against his New Testament and ordered its destruction, was now forced to swim with the stream, and the third

---
[1] See Stoughton for Illustration.

edition bears on its title-page his name, as over-seeing the translation by the king's command. By a specified day this complete English Bible was to be set up in every church throughout the kingdom. Latimer ordered it to be chained in the monastery of Worcester. Bonner put six copies in St. Paul's, and was sore distressed to find that people persisted in reading them even during the public services and while the preacher was declaring the word of God. Crowds would gather about the book, which was chained to a pillar, and there would be eager discussions as to the meaning of the passages read aloud by some scholar who chanced to be present.[1]

A. D. 1540.

This bright hour was destined to be very brief. Cromwell's execution removed the principal advocate for the English Bible from the counsels of the king. In 1543, Henry's mind had completely changed. Tyndale's translation was prohibited by Act of Parliament. Coverdale's ambition to see a Bible published with his annotations was dashed to the ground by a clause commanding that all Bibles thus accompanied should be destroyed. Neither in public nor in private were apprentices, artificers, journeymen, servants, husbandmen, and laborers to be permitted to read the Scriptures. The public reading in the churches by the curates was probably continued, but the tide had set in against

---

[1] Eadie, Vol. I., pp. 400, 401.

the English Bible, and no one could tell how far or how fast it would run. Happily Henry VIII. was drawing near his end; but Coverdale's heart must have sunk when   d., A. D. 1547. the sovereign to whom he had been so loyal issued another proclamation, in 1546, coupling his own version with that of Tyndale in a common condemnation. The bishops who had put their names to it, now hastened to disown their signatures. In some places Bibles were burned. The last edition of the Great Bible printed in Henry's reign appeared in 1541. A half-hearted proposition for a new translation fell to the ground. Coverdale himself fled to the continent, and in the town of Bergzabern married, was pastor of a church, and kept school.[1] On the 28th of January, 1547, Henry died, and the period of suspense came to an end.

The accession of Edward VI., brought Coverdale home again. He was made a royal chaplain, and his zeal in suppressing a revolt in the west of England was rewarded with the bishopric of Exeter. The work of revision, however, if it did not actually slumber during the brief reign of the frail young king, was not active. The bishops were busy giving a constitution and prayer book to the English church. Cranmer, who never lost sight of the supreme ambition of his life, appointed

---
[1] Dore, p. 89.

two great scholars, Fagius and Bucer, to professorships at Cambridge, and laid upon them the task of interpreting the Scriptures "according to the propriety of the language," and of illustrating obscure passages and reconciling those which seemed to be at variance the one with the other. But Fagius and Bucer both fell sick, and this, as the old chronicler, Strype, says: "gave a very unhappy stop to their studies." That the demand for the Scriptures grew is proved by the fact that, although Edward reigned only six years and a half, thirteen editions of Bibles and thirty-five of Testaments were published in England during his reign. The most ambitious attempt at a new version was made by Sir John Cheke, at one time professor of Greek at Cambridge, and tutor to Edward VI. He completed the Gospel of Matthew and began Mark; but then his work ceased. Possibly it was never intended for publication. Cheke had a perverse ingenuity in coining words, preferring *biword*, to parable; *gainbirth*, to regeneration; *uprising*, to resurrection; *freshmen*, to proselytes; *crossed*, to crucified.[1]

A. D. 1547-1553.

In 1553, the young king, from whom the Protestant party had hoped to receive such great benefits, passed away. Queen Mary at once prohibited the open reading of the Scriptures, and copies which

---

[1] Westcott, pp. 119, 120.

had been set up in the churches were burnt, but so deep and strong was the popular feeling in favor of the Bible in the vernacular, that no vigorous effort was made to find and forfeit the copies which must have been hidden away in thousands of English homes.

Not long after her accession to the throne, Mary, accompanied by her husband, Philip of Spain, passed in procession through the gayly decked streets of London. Among the emblematic designs which welcomed them was one representing her royal father, Henry VIII., giving a Bible to his young son, Edward. Perhaps it had appeared before when Edward visited the city. Times were changed now, however, and the artist was summoned before Bishop Gardiner, branded as "a villain and traitor," and bidden paint out the book and put a glove in its place. Evidently England was no country for Protestants. Cranmer and Rogers were burned. The bones of Fagius and Bucer were treated in the same way. Coverdale was imprisoned, and only escaped martyrdom by the special intervention of the king of Denmark. John Macbee, a Scotch minister living in Denmark, married to Coverdale's sister, had the ear of the sovereign, and welcomed the exile when once again he sought a shelter from persecution in his own country.

The next trace we have of him is in Geneva,

and it was during this period of forced absence from England that Coverdale, together with William Whittingham, who was related by marriage to Calvin, and other exiles prepared the version of the Bible which gained and held the heart of the English people for the next half-century. The Genevan Testament appeared in 1557, and Calvin himself prefaced it with an "Introductory Epistle." In size and price it was better fitted than the Great Bible for general circulation, and Coverdale must have seen with satisfaction the addition of the marginal commentary, on which his heart had been set in his earlier work. No sooner was the Testament published than the learned exiles plunged into the more serious business of revising the whole Bible. They continued at their task "for the space of ten years and more, day and night." Before they had concluded it, Mary died, and Elizabeth ascended the English throne. Coverdale seems to have gone home, but under the care of Whittingham, with one or two more who remained awhile in Geneva, the work of revision was thoroughly completed. With a dedication "to the most virtuous and noble Queen Elizabeth, whom God hath made our Zerubbabel for the erecting of this most excellent Temple," the Genevan Bible made its appearance in 1560. In form it was a moderate quarto; for the first time the text was

A. D. 1557.

A. D. 1560.

printed in Roman letter, and the chapters were divided into verses. For the first time also the Apocrypha was omitted. The monopoly of printing it was granted by Elizabeth to John Bodley, whose name lives still in the famous library at Oxford. Eighty editions appeared before the Authorized Version came to dispute with it the place of honor in the affections of the country.

It was on August 24, 1559, that a bishop from England,[1] no doubt Coverdale, requested a dismissal from the city council of Geneva, so that he might return to England. He never resumed his bishopric, but was given the living of St. Magnus' Church, near London Bridge. "Surely," said the bishop of London, in pleading that higher honors should be paid to him, "it is not well that he, *qui ante nos omnes fuit in Christo* should be now, in his age, without stay of living." He was very poor. During his exile he had been described as "a poor pilgrim," and now he was unable to pay the queen the firstfruits of his benefice. Being "not like to live a year," he pathetically appeals to his sovereign for her bounty. In 1566, he resigned his living, and soon after, at the advanced age of eighty-one, he died. A. D. 1569.

Compared with Wycliffe and Tyndale, Miles Coverdale may seem to lack in force of character and in independence. A courtier with Cromwell,

---
[1] Stoughton, p. 201.

he became a Puritan with Calvin. He trusted—as his predecessors in the work of translation did not —to royal patronage, to the favor of statesmen, and to the inspiration of his ecclesiastical superiors. No doubt he aimed at obtaining for his work the king's most gracious license. No doubt he caught quickly the impress of the hour. But, we must remember that he made no profession of originality, and contented himself by assuring the reader that if he was fervent in prayer God would discover to him the nobler services of Tyndale, and also move others to attach themselves to the good work in which he was content to be an obscure laborer.[1]

His life was everywhere simple and beautiful. When he had means at his disposal, he was profuse in his hospitality. In his fair old age he loved to preach, and people loved to listen to him. They "ran after Father Coverdale," we are told, and would call at his house to ask where he would preach the next Lord's Day. To him alone belongs the distinction of giving a whole Bible to the English nation. In his faith in the gospel he wavered as little as he did in his faith in the Scriptures, and when he died the English Reformation was already an accomplished fact, and the English Bible was secured forever to the English people.

---

[1] Westcott, p. 75.

V.

THE BISHOPS' BIBLE.

I utterly dissent from those who are unwilling that the Sacred Scriptures should be read by the unlearned, translated into their vulgar tongue, as though Christ had taught such subtleties that they can scarcely be understood even by a few theologians, or as though the strength of the Christian religion consisted in men's ignorance of it.—*Erasmus*.

CHAPTER V.

QUEEN ELIZABETH AND THE BISHOPS' BIBLE.

TYNDALE, the young student, aspired to see the Bible in the hands of English ploughboys. Tyndale the martyr did not die before the ambition to which he had surrendered his whole life was gratified. He perished at the stake a year after Coverdale's Bible appeared. In his turn, Coverdale was possessed of a purpose which to his mind seemed not less worthy than Tyndale's. His desire was to have an English Bible sent forth with the authority of "The king's most gracious licence," and under the auspices of the leaders of the Established Church. The year before he died this desire also was gratified. The Bishops' Bible was published in 1568. Its title declared that it was authorized by the ecclesiastical authorities, and the printer loudly claimed for it the sanction of the sovereign.   A.D.1568.

By this time Elizabeth had been queen of England ten years, and the people had no excuse for ignorance as to the policy which she proposed to pursue. More than any other of her house, she had the qualities which made that house so great. She united the cautious shrewdness of Henry VII., her grandfather, and the lavish splendor of her father, Henry VIII. As well as either of them she knew how to keep the word of promise to the ear and break it to the hope.

A Protestant at heart she certainly was not, but she was as firmly resolved as was her royal father before her, to have no foreign prince, secular or sacred, lording it over England. She was supreme in her own realm, and there can be no question that the passionate devotion with which she inspired the bravest and noblest of her courtiers, fairly expressed the loyalty of the people at large.

The concessions which she made to the Protestant party at the commencement of her reign only restored to that party the liberties granted by Edward VI. In every parish church a copy "of the whole Bible of the largest volume," was to be set up once more ; and "with great humility and reverence, as the very lively word of God," all were to read the same.

As she rode in royal state through London, Father Time appeared in the pageant leading his white-robed daughter, Truth. In her hand she carried the English Bible, which she presented to Elizabeth, who laid it upon her breast, heartily thanking the city for their present and promising often to read it. The assurance was all the more welcome because her people were in no little doubt as to the ardor of her Protestant convictions. In

his collection of apothegms, Lord Bacon writes:
"On the morrow of her coronation, it being the
custom to release prisoners at the inauguration of
a prince, ... one of her courtiers ... besought
her with a loud voice, 'That now this good time
there might be four or five principal prisoners
more released; these were the four evangelists and
the Apostle St. Paul, who had been long shut up
in an unknown tongue, as it were in prison, so as
they could not converse with the common people.'
The Queen answered very gravely, 'That it was
best first to inquire whether they
would be released or no.'"[1] Par- A. D. 1559-1575.
ker, the archbishop of Canterbury, who with no
little of Cranmer's tact inherited much of Cranmer's zeal for revision, would lose no opportunity
for assuring her majesty on this point. The need
was urgent for a version of the Bible at once
authoritative and popular. Ecclesiastical patronage and protection had failed to make for the Great
Bible any permanent place in England. It remained chained in the church, but the Genevan
Version was at home at the fireside. In a letter to
Secretary Cecil, written in 1565,[2] Parker of Canterbury, and Edmund Grindal, bishop of London,

---

[1] Bacon's "Apothegms," p. 4.

[2] Cecil was himself invited to take part in the translation, "that ye may be one of the builders of this good work in Christ's church." —Dore, p. 237.

mark out the policy which they proposed to pursue in dealing with the popular Bible, by promising that if Bodley's patent for printing it might be extended twelve years longer, they would see to it "that no impression should pass but by their direction, consent, and advice." So well did they keep their promise that it was not until the archbishop's death that the version was published in England itself. Nothing, however, could check the popularity of the Genevan Bible with the people. For three-quarters of a century it held its place as the household Bible of the English speaking nations.[1]

It could scarcely be expected that a good Anglican would feel very kindly toward the Genevan Bible. In its marginal annotations no measured terms were used when the opportunity occurred for launching a missile against prelacy. By the word "bishop" the apostle was said to mean only pastors, doctors, and elders; "deacons" were simply almoners of the bounty of the church to the poor and sick. When Paul spoke of "beggarly elements," he had in his mind ceremonies in worship, in which Easter and Whitsuntide might be included. In common with so many commentators, strongly influenced by their times, the Genevan divines reveled in the Apocalypse, and saw in the locusts "worldly prelates . . . with

---

[1] Westcott, 126.

archbishops, bishops, etc.," and in the crown which the locusts wore, the proud titles in which the priests boasted themselves, but "which in deede belongeth nothing unto them."[1]

Apart from these personal considerations which placed the bishops on the horns of a dilemma between a version which the people loved but which they themselves could not approve, and a version which they sanctioned but which the people would not use, it is easy to see that uniformity was peremptorily demanded in the interests of truth. In this church the Great Bible was used, in that the Genevan. The minds of the people would be distracted and torn over the rival claims of Lambeth and Geneva. On the very field where all parties should be united, the fiercest battle would be fought. Very early in Elizabeth's reign, a bill was enacted "for reducing of diversities of Bibles now extant in the English tongue to one settled vulgar, translated from the original."[2]

To the long and honorable line of men devoted to the publication of the English Bible we now add another name. The task of planning the new version could scarcely have fallen into hands better fitted to carry it through with credit than those of Archbishop Parker. Of full and ripe scholarship, happily constituted to bear the numberless petty annoyances to which such a leader would be

---

[1] Edgar, p. 192.   [2] Stoughton, p. 208.

exposed, impartial enough to admire the Genevan Bible while conscious of its ecclesiastical bias, with a certain adroit good humor coupled with genuine kindliness of heart, Parker was far too genuine a man to merit the caricature which Butler draws of him in "Hudibras." But he is lampooned by the satirist in honorable company. The creature of the vices of the court in London and of the virulence of the Vatican at Rome may be excused for failing to recognize the conspicuous virtue of either Anglican or Puritan. Four years (1564–68) were devoted to the preparation of the Bishops' Bible. "The archbishop 'sorted out the whole Bible into parcels,' and distributed these for examination and revision among qualified divines.'"[1] His own biblical studies fitted him to be himself the final arbitrator on all points of dispute raised by his staff. The copy of instructions which he sent to each reviser advises that the new version should be based on the Great Bible, while the work of other translators was to be respected, and no alterations made save for sufficient reason. The revisers were to "make no bitter notes upon any text nor yet set down any determination in places of controversy." Words which usage or fashion had now decided to be light or indelicate were to be changed for "more convenient terms or phrases."

Although initials are placed at the end of some

· Edgar, p. 195.

of the books, a complete list of the contributors is nowhere given. Of the revisers who can be probably identified, eight were bishops, and from them the revision derived its popular title.[1]

The archibishop's suavity must have been severely taxed during his four years of superintendence. Some of the revisers seem themselves to have stood in need of revision. Cox, bishop of Ely, writing to Parker on the subject of the "Psalms," suggested that "the translation of the verbs be used uniformly in one tense," and we can forgive the unconscious humor of the historian who remarks: "The archibishop accordingly gave to this prelate Acts and Romans."[2] Evidently he might better be trusted with Greek than with Hebrew. Guest, bishop of Rochester, had no hesitation in turning "the præter-perfect tense into the present tense, because the sense is too harsh in the præter-perfect tense," and he is so determined that the quotations from the Old Testament, which are found in the New, shall be correctly made that he adopts the following principle: "When in the New Testament one piece of a psalm is reported I translate it in the Psalms according to the translation thereof in the New Testament, for the avoiding of the offense that may rise to the people upon divers translations." Whatever may be said of the morality of this canon there can be no question

---

[1] Westcott, p. 135.   [2] Edgar, p. 199.

that it is extremely simple, and were it universally adopted a vast amount of controversy would no doubt be avoided.

Certainly Bishop Cox, although not to be trusted with Hebrew verbs, hit the mark when he wrote to Parker: "I perceive the greatest burden will lie upon your neck touching care and travail." The result was just what might have been anticipated. The Old Testament was inferior in its execution to the New; both were unequal in merit, and as Professor Moulton says: "The verdict of the student will vary according to the portion which he is examining." The Great Bible is followed most closely in the historical books of the Old Testament, and throughout that version is preferred to the Genevan, sometimes with advantage, but more frequently without. The influence of Tyndale is strongly felt, and notwithstanding Parker's recommendation there are numerous instances in which inelegant words and phrases remain. The variations from previous versions are more numerous in the New Testament than in the Old, and Bishop Westcott, on a critical analysis of one passage (Eph. 4:7-16), decides that "the character of the original correction marks very close and thoughtful revision, based faithfully upon the Greek."

The notes in the Bishops' Bible, while avoiding the controversial bitterness which the good archbishop deprecated, are such as might as a rule have emanated from Geneva, and their sturdy Protestantism is often worthy of Luther himself. The printer and engraver did their utmost to produce a volume deserving of the place which the new Bible was intended to fill. It was issued in magnificent style, profusely ornamented with wood engravings; embellished in questionable taste with copper-plate portraits of the queen, Leicester, and Burleigh ; furnished with a map of Palestine ; and supplemented by an elaborate series of genealogical tables.

Besides translating "Genesis," "Exodus," the first two Gospels, and most of the Epistles of Paul, and, adding as Strype says, "the last hand," and caring for the printing and publishing of the whole, Archbishop Parker wrote on behalf of the revisers two prefaces, one for the Old and the other for the New Testament. In these he exults on account of the rich legacy which "not in promise but in open sight," the believer inherits. There may indeed, he confesses, be dark places yet, but the gifts and graces of the Holy Spirit flow as continually and abundantly as from the beginning, and "who can doubt but that such things as remain yet unknown in the gospel shall be hereafter made open to the later wits of our posterity, to their clear understanding."[1]

---

[1] Westcott, p. 134.

A patent was granted to Richard Jugge to publish the Bishops' Bible *cum priviligio Regiæ majestatis*. This was partially renewed to his son John; but in 1579, Christopher Barker, by paying a great sum, purchased the exclusive right to issue Bibles and Testaments in the English tongue, and although with varying fortune, this monopoly was retained by the Barkers until the year 1709.[1]

Parker and Cecil united to urge the merits of the new version on the attention of Queen Elizabeth, but she does not seem to have granted her royal sanction to it, although Convocation which would scarcely have run counter to her pleasure, approved it heartily. Every archbishop and bishop was ordered to have a large paper copy in his house, and to place it in the hall or dining room for the special use of servants and strangers. No cathedral must be without it, and as far as convenient, churches should be furnished with it also.

Yet the Bishops' Bible was never popular. It did indeed succeed in supplanting the Great Bible in the churches, but the Genevan Bible was still the people's choice. Thirteen editions of Parker's Version appeared in folio, one in octavo, six in quarto. The small-sized edition, printed in 1584, was sufficient to meet the demands for it which came from the hearthstones of England; but sixteen such editions of the Genevan Version were

---
[1] Eadie, Vol. II., chapter 48.

published between 1611 and 1688, while fifty-two in quarto and eighteen in folio, confirm us in the belief that even the halls and churches in many instances preferred the Bible of the exiles to the Bible of the ecclesiastics. Although "set forth by authority," the authority was only that of Convocation, and even those who should have been obedient to their spiritual superiors seem to have faltered in their loyalty. Nine years after its publication the archbishop complains that the churches are not sufficiently furnished with Bibles, while many have to put up with copies torn, defaced, and "not of the translation authorized by the synod of bishops."[1] No doubt there was still a Romish, as well as a Puritan sentiment strong in England, and the Bishops' Bible satisfied neither the one nor the other. The original views as to translation held by some of the revisers did not impart distinction to its pages. It was voted timid, and therefore colorless. Although Bishop Cox argued against "ink-horn terms," the English of the people was often sacrificed for stale, stilted phraseology. The music of David fares badly in such a rendering as, *God is my shephearde, therefore I can lack nothyng : he will cause me to repose myself in pastures full of grasse, and he will leade me into calme waters;* and the pithiness of the original evaporates in the translation of Pro-

---

[1] Edgar, p. 196.

verbs 25 : 27, *Curiously to search the glory of heavenly things is not commendable;* while the fantastic spirit which delights in quips drove Paul from the field in the words, *I thought it necessary to exhort the brethren that they should come before unto you, and prepare your fore-promised beneficence, that it might be ready as a beneficence, and not as an extortion.*[1]

That the Bishops' Bible failed to gain the hearts of the people, or even the adherence of the clergy, and repels the respect of scholars, is little to be wondered at. The close of Elizabeth's reign saw rival versions still in possession. In addition to the Genevan Version, with its obnoxious controversial comment, there was the Rheims New Testament, which reached England in 1582, carefully guarding itself against the supposition that it was intended for "ale-benches, boats, and barges," and aiming to keep close to the "authentic text of the Vulgate." It was the response given by the English Roman Catholic refugees in Rheims to a challenge to suspend criticisms of existing translations and produce a better themselves. The evening before her execution in Fotheringay Castle, Mary, Queen of Scots, swore her innocence upon this book, and when the Earl of Kent objected that the book itself was false, she answered, quickly : "Does your lordship believe that my oath would be better if I

---

[1] Edgar, p. 225.

swore on your translation, in which I do not believe?"[1] The Old Testament, under the same auspices, was published at Douay, in 1609, having been delayed, as the editors say, thirty years, "owing to their poor estate in banishment."

In addition to the Rheims New Testament, a translation from Beza's Latin version of the book had been made by Lawrence Tomson, an undersecretary to Sir Francis Walsingham; and a learned Hebraist, Hugh Broughton, dissatisfied with the Bishops' Bible, and failing in securing the partnership of "six of the longest students in the tongues," in a scheme for producing a better, tried his own hand at the books of David, Ecclesiastes, Lamentations, and Job. Although his overbearing temper made him an impracticable coadjutor, yet upon the royal version, when that came to be executed, his independent labors had a perceptible influence.

Thus matters stood when Elizabeth died. The history of the English Bible from the dawning with Wycliffe to the final labors of Archbishop Parker, covers a period of almost two hundred years. We have now followed the changing fortunes of the book thus far. The days have forever passed in which it can be banned and banished, and those who read it tortured and burned. The fiercest opponents to its free circulation have themselves sent

---

[1] Eadie, Vol. 2, p. 136.

forth English New Testaments from their own place of exile. The leaders of the Established Church are now united in their resolve to have one version uniformly employed. Twice the primate of England has thrown himself into an enterprise to which scholarship, authority, and even royal favor have lent their weight and influence. And yet the enterprise, in each instance, has failed. The people have persisted in making their own choice, and it has been a choice adverse to the bishops. But now at last, the hour has come when a version of the English Bible can be prepared in obedience to the command of the crown, and by the hands of the ecclesiastical leaders of the State, which shall win its way to the hearts and homes of the people at large.

VI.

THE AUTHORIZED VERSION.

"Therefore, blessed be they, and most honored be their name that break the ice, and give the onset upon that which helpeth forward to the saving of souls. Now what can be more available thereto than to deliver God's book unto God's people in a tongue which they can understand?"—*Preface to King James' Bible.*

CHAPTER VI.

THE AUTHORIZED VERSION.

IN the year 1603, James I. came riding up to London to be crowned king of England. His progress from Scotland, with its pageants in the towns and villages through which he passed, and the opportunity to enjoy hunting in the parks and forests of the nobles, must have been a welcome change from the narrow life to which he had been accustomed. At Wilton, however, he found time in his intervals from sport to consider the complaints of the Puritans, who appealed to him to deliver them and the national church from the tyranny of their rivals, the Ritualists. With the exception of hunting, there was nothing which James enjoyed more than a theological controversy. It pleased him to think himself superior to the divines in their own domain. The prospect of a religious discussion between the two contending parties, in which he should play the part of umpire, caught his pedantic fancy. He so far listened to the petition of the Puritans, as to appoint a conference at Hampton Court, at which their grievances should be considered. The A.D. 1604. date fixed was the January following; but probably before that time had come the Puritans knew that they had little to hope for from the prince, who, if he was born in the country of Knox, was himself the son of Knox's bitterest enemy. James gave the conference plainly to understand that his sympathies were with the High Church party, and that he was resolved to suppress all differences of opinion and to maintain "one doctrine, one discipline, and one religion in substance and ceremony."

Yet, looking at the event from this distance, we can see how the Puritans came off from an apparently bootless mission with great spoil. Their representative, Dr. Reynolds, President of Corpus Christi College, Oxford, raised the question of a revision of the Scriptures. A new translation of the Bible was needed, he said, because "those which were allowed in the reigns of King Henry VIII. and Edward VI. were corrupt and not answerable to the truth." This statement he supported by various quotations from the Great Bible and the Bishops' Bible. What, for example, could be made of the words: "Mount Sinai is Agar in Arabia, and bordereth upon the city which is now called Jerusalem"? Paul never said that. It was a travesty of his teaching in Gal. 4 : 25. And why were they forced to read in church "They were not obedient" (Ps. 105 : 28), when the Psalter said the very reverse? And why was Ps. 106 : 30 translated "Then stood up Phinehas and prayed," when the original ran, "*and executed judgment*"? Reynolds' objections to the versions then in use were bluntly met by Bancroft, bishop of London, who broke in: "If every man's humour is to be followed, there will be no end of translations." No doubt much to the bishop's chagrin, the king sided with the Puritans in this one instance, although he contrived to insult their prejudices even while he fell in with their proposal: "I have never yet," said he, "seen a Bible well translated into English, and the worst of all the translations I have seen is the Geneva."[1] He favored one uniform translation. Let the universities prepare it, the church dignitaries revise it, the Privy Council approve it, and then he would himself give to it his royal authority, so the whole church should be bound to it and to none other. "But," he added, "let there be no marginal notes." An English lady had given him a copy of the Geneva Bible, and the notes he found full of lurking treason against the powers that be.

This happened, as we have said, in January, 1604. Convocation met in March, but nothing was done. The church leaders, as is not unusual with them, were inclined to a policy of masterly inaction. Not so the king. Bancroft soon discovered that James was in earnest. By mid-

---
[1] Edgar, p. 288.

summer the scholars who were to be responsible for the task were chosen—how this was done does not appear—and the list was approved by the sovereign. Peace was about this time concluded with Spain, and Bancroft wrote to Cambridge that he was persuaded the king was happier in the prospect of a new translation of the Bible than even in the assurance that his most formidable opponent among the courts of Europe was reconciled to him.

The peace with Spain was celebrated on a Sunday, given up to rejoicing. There was a grand banquet and ball, and the king, with the Spanish ambassador, witnessed the baiting of bears and bulls. The other project was not so readily disposed of; but James was able by the end of July to write to Bancroft—now acting as archbishop of the vacant see of Canterbury—that he had "appointed certain learned men to the number of four and fifty to do the work." Besides these, the bishop was to consult the scholarly clergy in their dioceses, that so "our intended translation may have the help and furtherance of all our principal learned men within this our kingdom."

It is amusing to see how James managed the matter of remunerating the translators. He requested patrons of church preferments not to fill up vacancies until his pleasure had been consulted, and in this way "seven of the forty-seven translators were raised to Episcopal dignity, and more than twice seven were settled in other comfortable livings."[1] Their immediate expenses the king "was very ready of his most princely disposition to have borne, but some of my lords, as things now go, did hold it inconvenient." Consequently, the bishops and chapters were requested to contribute toward this work. For himself, he would be the patron of "this our intended translation," and would take pains to be "acquainted with every man's liberality." This arrangement is highly characteristic of James. He did none of the work, paid nothing toward its cost, and took to himself all the credit of it. As a fact, the bishops seemed to have followed the king's example rather than his precept. Nothing was subscribed, and all that the translators received was free entertainment when they met.

Although the king's letter announces that fifty-four revisers had been selected, it was probably owing to delay and unavoidable inability to serve that in the final list only forty-seven names appeared. Death may have arrested some in their purpose; for although the preliminaries were settled before the end of 1604, two whole years passed before the work was formally begun.

By 1607, however, the enterprise was fairly

---
[1] Westcott, p. 145.

launched. The forty-seven scholars were divided into six parties, and they met at Westminster, at Cambridge, and at Oxford, according to the plan indicated below.[1] The names of these men as we read them now are most of them names only; but a few of them live in our history as scholars, preachers, and theologians. All of them merit perpetual honor for carrying through the great achievement of the seventeenth century. Most distinguished of them all was Launcelot Andrewes, dean of Westminster, afterward bishop of Chichester, whose name stands at the head of the first list, a man of rich scholarship, master of fifteen languages, with a brilliant reputation as a preacher, and worthy of the praise of Milton, who dedicated to his memory one of his early elegies.

[1]

PLACE.	NUMBER OF REVISERS.	BOOKS.
	I. Old Testament.	
1. Westminster	10	Genesis to 2 Kings, incl.
2. Cambridge	8	1 Chron. to Eccles., incl.
3. Oxford	7	Isaiah to Malachi.
	II. The Apocrypha.	
4. Cambridge	7	
	III. New Testament.	
5. Oxford	8	The four Gospels, Acts, Apocalypse.
6. Westminster	7	Romans to Jude, incl.

How well he understood his royal master is seen in the story which the poet Waller tells about him. The king one day sitting at dinner with Andrewes and his brother bishop, Neale of Durham, inquired: "My lords, cannot I take my subjects' money when I want it, without all this formality in Parliament?" Neale answered the question first: "God forbid, sir, but you should; you are the breath of our nostrils." James turned to Andrewes, "Well, my lord, what say you?" But Andrewes excused himself from replying. "He had," he said, "no skill to judge of parliamentary cases." James would take no denial. "No put-off, my lord; answer me presently." "Then, sir," said he, "I think it lawful for you to take my brother Neale's money, for he offers it."

Reynolds, to whom we have already alluded as the leader of the Puritan party in the church, was one of the Old Testament committee at Oxford. It was at his house that they met to complete their portion, and he had the chief hand in this final revision, although "sorely afflicted with the gout." His prodigious learning, in the extravagant language of his contemporaries, placed him above all writers—profane, ecclesiastical, and divine; and also above all the councils of the church. He was more diligent than even Origen; and of him, as of Athanasius, it might be said that "to name Reynolds is to commend virtue itself."

Reynolds died before the completion of the work, and so did Lively, a very accomplished scholar, "our Hebrew reader in Cambridge," on whom the king had especially relied for assistance. Although the formal work of the translators did not begin before 1607, yet the fact of Lively's death in 1605, after something had been done, lends color to the belief that the more enthusiastic scholars started work much earlier. Fuller, the church historian, says as much, and adds that the rest "vigorously, though slowly proceeded in this hard, heavy, and holy task; nothing offended with the censures of impatient people condemning their delays — though indeed but due deliberation — for laziness."[1]

Certainly Bois, of Cambridge, could not have exposed himself to the charge of indolence, for he only subtracted time to return to his parish every Saturday night, and by Monday morning was at his task again; when he had finished his own portion he undertook that of another scholar to whom it had been assigned, and after four years of incessant labor he formed one of the band of six who finally revised the whole at Stationers' Hall, London. In three-quarters of a year their crowning work was completed, and Bois could return to his parish again. The Stationers' Company, probably interested in the profits of the printing, paid

---

[1] Stoughton, pp. 247, 248.

him and his five companions thirty shillings a week for the last revision, and this pitiful sum seems to have been all that they received in return for nearly five years' hard work.

Returning to the lists once more, we notice the singular richness of the universities in Hebraists. Six professors of Hebrew were engaged in revision, besides Bedwell, the most distinguished Arabic scholar of the time, and Bois, who was especially famous for Oriental learning.[1] "No doubt can be entertained," says Westcott, "as to the ability and acquirements of the revisers." If Cecil refused to take a layman's share in the Bishops' Bible, the Authorized Version had the advantage of the assistance of the accomplished provost of Eton, Sir Henry Savile, while the name of a Frenchman, D. A. de Sararia, an expert modern linguist, preserves the fame of the only foreigner engaged in the work. Dr. John Layfield was especially skilled in architecture; Dr. Thomas Holland was mighty in the Scriptures; Kilbye "had Hebrew at his fingers' ends"; and Miles Smith was to compose the fulsome dedication to the king and be rewarded with the bishopric of Gloucester for this elaborate specimen of courtly imagination. Selden, in his "Table-Talk," sketches the various bands at their work, in Westminster and the two universities. We

---
[1] Westcott, pp. 149, 150.

can see them as we read his graphic words: "That part of the Bible was given to him who was most excellent in such a tongue ; and then they met together, and one read the translation, the rest holding in their hands some Bible, either of the learned tongues, or French, Spanish, Italian, etc. If they found any fault they spoke, and if not, he read on." When a portion had been thus gone over it was sent to the rest for their approval, and either passed or referred to the committee on final revision, through whose hands every chapter and verse went before the printers received it.

The instructions which Bancroft, by the king's orders, sent to each one of the revisers, are well worthy of study. They afford the amplest proof of the thoroughness with which the work was planned. The Bishops' Bible was to be followed with as little alteration as the truth of the original would permit : proper names were to be retained "as nigh as may be accordingly as they were vulgarly used"; old ecclesiastical terms were to be kept—*church*, for instance, was not to be translated *congregation;* where one word had different significations that one was to be kept which had the authority of the Fathers, so long as it was agreeable to the propriety of the place and the analogy of faith ; the divisions of the chapters were to be left as far as possible as they were ; except to explain the Hebrew or Greek, no marginal notes

The prologge.

I haue here translated (brethern and susters moost dere and tenderly beloued in Christ) the newe Testament for youre spirituall edyfyinge / consolacion / and solas: Exhortynge instantly and besechynge those that are better sene in the tonge then y / and that haue hyer gyftes of grace to interpret the sence of the scripture / and meanynge of the spyrite / then y /to consydre and pondre my laboure / and that with the spyrite of mekenes. And yf they perceyve in eny places that y haue not attayned the very sence of the tonge / or meanynge of the scripture / or haue not geven the right englysshe worde / that they put to there handes to amende it /remembrynge that so is there duetie to doo. For we haue not receyved the gyftes of god for oure selues only /or for to hyde them: but for to bestowe them vnto the honouringe of god and christ / and edyfyinge of the congregacion /wchich is the body of christ.

¶ The causes that moved me to translate /y thought better that other shulde ymagion /then that y shulde rehearce them. More over y supposed yt superfluous / for who ys so blynde to axe why lyght shulde be shewed to them that walke in dercknes / where they cannot but stomble /and where to stomble ys the daunger of eternall dammacion / other so despyghtfull that he wolde envye eny man (y speake nott his brother) so necessary a thinge / or so bedlem madde to affyrme that good is the naturall cause of ynell /and derknes to procede oute of lyght / and that lyinge shulde be grounded in trougth and veryte / and nott rather clene contrary / that lyght destroyeth dercknes /and veritie reproveth all manner lyinge.

were to be affixed; such quotations of places as served for the fit reference of one Scripture to another were to be put in the margin; each man was first of all to do his work by himself; then all of the company were to meet and compare results; and finally each company was to send the book complete to the rest to be considered seriously and judiciously. On this point "his majesty is very careful." Then followed the provision already mentioned for a final revision of the whole. Proceeding, the instructions provide that obscure passages should be submitted to learned men outside the companies of the revisers, such men being sought out by the bishops. The deans of Westminster and Chester were to direct the company at Westminster, the professors of Hebrew and Greek occupying the post in the universities. The translations of Tyndale, Matthew, Coverdale, Whitchurch (substantially the same as the Great Bible), and the Genevan versions were to be used where they were found to be truer to the original than the Bishops' Bible. Finally, to meet a difficulty as suggested by the rule as to translating words of different significance, three or four of the most ancient and grave divines in the universities were to oversee the work in conference with the directors of the companies, so that full and fair justice might be done to the fathers and to the analogy of faith.

Dr. Miles Smith has atoned for his dedication to James, with its offensive adulation of that most high and mighty Prince, by an "Address to the Reader," which remains to us still as one of the noblest compositions of the age when our English tongue was at its best. The printers, doing the thing which they ought not to do, and leaving undone the thing that they should do, have removed this preface from our modern editions of the Bible, although until quite lately they have persisted in printing the epistle dedicatory to the king. To us it is valuable as the only existing account of the labors of the revisers. Contrasting their deliberate course with the traditional haste with which the Septuagint was prepared, Dr. Smith says of the new book that "it hath not been huddled up in seventy-two days, but hath cost the workmen, as light as it seemeth, the pains of twice seven times seventy-two days, and more." He acknowledges the labor of previous translators, both in England and beyond seas, owning that God had raised them up to do their good work, and saying that "they deserve to be held of us and of posterity in everlasting remembrance." In one or other of them the true rendering might be found, and in this new setting whatever is sound "will shine as gold more brightly, being rubbed and polished." The revisers had never dreamed of making a new translation, nor yet to make of a bad one a good one, but rather to make a good one better, and from all to compile a Bible not justly to be excepted against. This had been their endeavor and work. Consequently they had consulted the translators and commentators in all languages—Chaldee, Hebrew, Syriac, Greek, Latin, Spanish, French, Italian, and German. Nor did they disdain to revise what they had done, but brought back to the anvil that which they had hammered. They had used prayer as Augustine used it, crying : "Oh, let thy Scriptures be my pure delight ; let me not be deceived in them, neither let me deceive by them." With this purpose, and in this spirit had they met together, "not too many, lest one should trouble another ; and yet many, lest many things haply might escape them." So using all needful helps, not caring for the charge of slowness, nor coveting praise for expedition, they conclude by declaring in the same spirit of brave humility which had distinguished them from the beginning, "We have at length, through the good hand of the Lord upon us, brought the work to that pass that you see."

The revised version, newly translated out of the original tongues, and with the former translations diligently compared and revised by his majesty's special command, appeared in 1611. Richard Barker was the printer, paying well for the perpetual right.[1] The print-

A. D. 1611.

---
[1] Stoughton, p. 236.

ing of the Bishops' Bible had virtually ceased when the authorized Bible was undertaken. The weight of ecclesiastical authority was given exclusively to the new version. It was appointed to be read in churches. The favor of the king would naturally be accorded to a work which he himself had planned, and his inordinate vanity would find no difficulty in believing that his literary fame had indeed reached "the farthest parts of Christendom," while the church recognized in him her most tender and loving nursing-father, and the nation at large saw in him that "sanctified person who under God was the immediate author of its true happiness."[1]

And yet, after so much royal and ecclesiastical patronage had been bestowed upon it, we are surprised to learn that "no evidence has yet been produced to show that the version has ever been publicly sanctioned by Convocation, or by Parliament, or by the Privy Council, or by the king."[2]

The critics were soon in the field tilting at it after their usual fashion. Poor Hugh Broughton, disappointed in his private enterprise, declared that the new version bred in him a sadness which would grieve him while life lasted. ".It is," said he, "so ill done." He assured the king that he would rather be torn in pieces by wild horses than see it urged on the churches. The witch

---
[1] "Epistle Dedicatory."   [2] Westcott, p. 158.

mania, which soon after this time sent its disastrous consequences even into New England, was already in the air, and the translators were accused of giving in to the superstition of the king in their use of such words as "familiar spirit," "witch," and "wizard." Kilbye, the learned Hebraist, who had sat in the Oxford company, happening one day to worship in a village church in Derbyshire, was amused when the young preacher—ignorant that one of the revisers was among his hearers—inveighed against the translation of several words, and in the case of one which seems to have been especially objectionable to him, gave three reasons why it ought to have been differently rendered. After the evening service the doctor had his revenge, telling the preacher that he had wasted his opportunity with the poor people in his congregation. As to his three reasons, he and his colleagues "had considered all of them, and found thirteen more considerable reasons why it was translated as now printed."[1]

With more serious objections to the Authorized Version we shall concern ourselves in a later chapter. For the present, it is sufficient to say that before fifty years had passed it had won its way to the hearts of the English people, not so much because the king, the bishops, and the universities lent it the sanction of their august

---
[1] Walton's "Lives."—*Sanderson.*

names, as because it was intrinsically superior to all others. Even the Genevan Version gradually disappeared. The fickle fortunes of the house of Stuart waxed and waned. Long after his dynasty had vanished, the praises of James perplexed the boys and girls in the parish churches when they relieved the dullness of the sermon by poring over the famous dedication. For two centuries and a half the Bible of King James continued to merit the praise of Selden, the great lawyer: "The English translation of the Bible is the best translation in the world, and renders the sense of the original best." Designed for public reading, it still answers its end admirably, and for majesty and sweetness will never be rivalled, certainly never surpassed. "It lives on the ear like a music that can never be forgotten; like the sound of church bells. Its felicities often seem to be things rather than words. It is part of the national mind, and the anchor of national seriousness."[1]

---

[1] Faber

VII.

BETWEEN THE VERSIONS.

"Translation it is that openeth the window, to let in the light; that breaketh the shell, that we may eat the kernel; that putteth aside the curtain, that we may look into the most holy place."—*Preface to King James' Bible.*

CHAPTER VII.

BETWEEN THE VERSIONS.

IF the success of King James' Bible was not immediate, it was no doubt as rapid as the revisers expected. Their knowledge of human nature made them as moderate in their expectations as they were modest in their claims. Welcomed with suspicion instead of love, and with emulation instead of thanks, "zeal to promote the common good found," they said, "but cold entertainment in the world." It was sure to be misconstrued, and in danger of being condemned; as would naturally be anticipated by those who turned either to history or to their own experience. The Commonwealth period was over before the Genevan Bible ceased to be the Bible of the homes, and in the churches the Bishops' Bible lingered in the remoter parishes until the beginning of the eighteenth century.[1]

Further revision was advocated in Parliament in 1645, and only the dissolution of the long Parliament prevented the passing of a bill providing for it. The project was supported by Owen, Cudworth, Goodwin, Caryl, and others scarcely less

---
[1] Edgar.

eminent for devoutness and learning. Happily the political crisis was not favorable to any further revision, and so the affections of the English people had time to twine about the book which in those dark and troublous times never failed while feeding their piety to foster their patriotism as well.

The advocates of an amended translation continued their agitation. Anglicans as well as Puritans were anxious for it. Of course they were not in the majority, otherwise the work would certainly have been attempted. The people at large were content with what they already had. The disposition of the Evangelical party, even in our own century, was to lay great stress on the power of the word, not only as one expression of the truth, but also as the *best* expression of the truth which could be found. Mr. Scrivener, in his valuable "Supplement to the Authorized English Version of the New Testament," trusts that it is not presumptuous to believe that God "guided the minds of the first editors in their selection of the authorities on which they rested."[1] Meanwhile, that the revision needed to be itself revised, was abundantly plain. Providence had not superintended the printers, nor had he endowed King James and his company with knowledge in advance of their times. The successive editions disproved

---

[1] "A Supplement to the Authorized English Version of the New Testament." Introduction, pp. 1-127.

any such claims. More than four hundred variations from the editions of 1611 appear in the edition of only three years later. In 1683, Dr. Scattergood carefully corrected the text; and a still more complete revision was carried through in 1769 by Dr. Blayney. It is to him that we are indebted for the marginal explanations of weights, measures and coins, and of Hebrew proper names; he amended the summaries of the Bible, and the running titles, and even ventured to correct some errors in the chronology. But advancing knowledge called for a work far more radical. There was a general belief that the Authorized Version failed in a multitude of instances to express the meaning of the original. The majority of these were of little moment, but popular rumor is sure to exaggerate, and rarely distinguishes. It was enough that the inaccuracies existed. The Cambridge paragraph Bible, 1873, gave a catalogue of the variations from the text of the Authorized Version as first published, which are now to be found in modern editions of the book, and the list occupied sixteen closely printed quarto pages. The Oxford Parallel Bible, 1885, made a selection from these deviations, and inserted them in their places in the margin.

While the royal patent prevented any invasion of the printer's monopoly, experiments in translation were continually appearing. An Authorized

Version seemed to be warranted by the independent translations which were continually appearing. The names of Purver, Macrae, Bellamy, Boothroyd, Doddridge, Macknight, Shairp, Thomson, Whiston, on the title-pages of various versions of the Old and New Testaments, were sufficient evidence that no one standard gave unity to the efforts of translators, who not infrequently indeed, represented conflicting doctrinal views. There was little uniformity of style either. The inflated taste of the period in which he lived made Doddridge prefer that the early believers should "partake of their refreshment"[1] rather than *eat their meat* (Acts 2 : 46), and that *the sincere milk of the word* (1 Peter 2 : 2) shall be known rather as milk "rational and unmingled." The rugged individuality of Macknight set aside the *corrupt communications* (Eph. 4 : 29) of the Authorized Version in favor of "rotten speech"; and declared that the words of Paul about marriage might fitly be rendered: "For this reason shall a man leave his father and mother, and shall be *glued* to his wife, and the two shall become one flesh" (Eph. 5 : 31). When it is added that in the century which preceded our present Revised Version twenty English translations of the New Testament were published, it may suggest itself to most minds that a careful and trustworthy revision of

---

[1] Edgar, p. 333.

the Bible was called for, if only to save the book from its friends.

The condition of critical scholarship as our century passed into its last quarter, was especially favorable to a revision of the New Testament. Already Alford, Ellicott, Lightfoot, Stanley, Farrar, had given us translations of the whole or of separate books. In America, which had taken its share in experimental versions, the scholarly labors of the Baptist American Bible Union had deepened the conviction that the hour had come when the whole Bible should be carefully revised, if not entirely re-translated.

To the question of revision we must now turn. There were many reasons why a revision should be carried through, but there were reasons not less numerous and even more weighty, why the Authorized Version should remain as the basis of any new enterprise.

What arguments, we may ask, favored a new version of the English Bible.

1. The first was based on an objection often urged to the principle adopted by the translators of King James' Version, of translating one Greek word by more than one English word. Thus *damnation*, *condemnation*, and in the margin, *judgment*, are translations of one Greek word only. *Eternal* and *everlasting* ; *impute*, *count*, and *account* ; *Comforter* and *Advocate* ; *covenant*

and *testament*, are additional illustrations of this unfortunate principle. The converse was equally disastrous. One and the same English word was used for many words in the original. *Conversation*, *devil*, *hell*, *tempt*, each represents two distinct words, and *ordain*, "an important word ecclesiastically and theologically," ten.[1]

2. Notwithstanding the constant revision to which the Authorized Version had been submitted, the condition of the punctuation, italics, and paragraphs, was still unsatisfactory. The many and conspicuous blunders of the original edition had indeed been corrected, but not a single Bible was printed which was not fairly exposed to serious objection.

3. Perhaps it was too much to hope that we should ever see a Bible absolutely without note or comment. It was not unreasonable, however, to demand that the headings of the chapters should not mislead the simple-minded reader, and that in the marginal references exegetical skill should not be set aside at the bidding of theological bias ; or, worse still, of erroneous principles of interpretation.

4. It was time that obsolete words should be dropped. There were not many of them, indeed, partly because the English of the Authorized Version was carefully chosen at the first, and partly

---

[1] "Brief Notes on the Critical History of the Text and English Version of Holy Scripture." Joseph Angus, M. A., D. D., p. 57.

because the version had itself embalmed words which might otherwise have fallen into oblivion. But there were few readers of the Bible who could tell what was done to the flax when it was *bolled* (Exod. 9 : 31). The peasant who knew a post only as "a thing that stood still to hang gates on or tie horses to," was puzzled to understand what Job meant when he said, *My days are swifter than a post*[1] (Job 9 : 25). Why did Herodias demand that the head of John the Baptist should be brought in *a charger* (Matt. 14 : 8), when the only charger known to the majority of people was a horse? and why did Paul and his companions *take up their carriages* and go to Jerusalem (Acts 21 : 15), when reason rather dictated that their carriages should take them?

5. Many forms of expression in the Authorized Version while at first admissible for their force, had in the lapse of time become unmusical if not unmeaning. That the early builders should say, *Go to, let us make brick* (Gen. 11 : 3); that a certain woman should cast a piece of millstone upon Abimelech's head *and all to brake his scull* (Judges 9 : 53); that of Moab it should be predicted, *with weeping shall they go it up* (Isa. 15 : 5), are cases in point. The use of *his* for *its*, *which* for *who*, *either* for *each*, *be* for *are*, also needed correction.

---

[1] Edgar, p. 371.

6. Occasionally there were translations which may perhaps have been clear to the translators themselves, but of which it was impossible for ordinary readers to make any sense. Especially was this so in the Old Testament. There are verses in Job and in the Prophets which convey no sort of meaning to the ear. *We have heard of the pride of Moab; he is very proud: even of his haughtiness, and his pride, and his wrath: but his lies shall not be so* (Isa. 16 : 6), illustrates this.[1]

7. To the objections to the old version which are founded on its language, we may add that a number of words which had not become obsolete had changed their meanings. "There are two hundred of them, and they affect the sense of many important passages." Among them are the following: *Apprehend, conversation, frankly, honest, let, mortify, piety, prevent, quick, religion, spoil, tale, tradition.*[2] In many instances these words and phrases conveyed a distinctly wrong thought to the mind of the reader. Numbers of devout students of the teachings of Jesus have been perplexed because he is reported to have said: *Take no thought for your life* (Matt. 6 : 25), when what he did say was, *Be not anxious for your life.* It was a fretful foreboding and not a prudent forecasting which our Lord forbade.

---

[1] Compare R. V., where the meaning is made clear.
[2] Angus, p. 53.

8. It was only reasonable to believe that the scholarship of the companies who met at Westminster, Oxford, and Cambridge, sound as it was, would not bear comparison with that of the nineteenth century. Much attention had been paid in the course of the intervening years to the ancient languages. The lexicons of to-day are more thorough and accurate, as well as more scientific in their arrangement, because greater attention has been given to the force of tenses, cases, articles, and prepositions. It might not have been theological bias so much as grammatical inaccuracy which wrote, *Such as should be saved* rather than *those that were being saved* (Acts 2 : 47).

9. The marginal notes in the first edition of the Authorized Version were nearly as numerous as the marginal references.[1] Those which suggested alternative readings might be considered afresh, and a conclusion arrived at as to their soundness. Should *They houghed an ox* take the place of *digged down a wall* (Gen. 49 : 6) ; and, *The north wind bringeth forth rain*, of *driveth away rain* (Prov. 25 : 23), and *I praise you, brethren, that you keep the traditions*, of *keep the ordinances* (1 Cor. 11 : 2) ; and was it not full time that we read *Eateth and drinketh* (not "*damnation*") but *judgment to himself?* (1 Cor. 11 : 29.)

10. Was it not time also that passages confess-

---

[1] Edgar, p. 323.

edly doubtful and probably spurious should be distinguished from those that were genuine? The touching story of the woman taken in adultery (John 8) was apparently a tradition—very likely with a basis of truth to it—which had crept into John's Gospel long after he wrote. In the account of the miracle at the pool of Bethesda (John 5) there were certainly verses whose later origin can scarcely be questioned. It was now generally although not universally believed that the last twelve verses of the Gospel of Mark (Mark 16 : 9–20) were not written by the evangelist. The doctrine of the Trinity did not stand in any need of the questionable support to be derived from the well known passage in John's first Epistle (1 John 5 : 7), which Tyndale, Coverdale, and the Great Bible placed in brackets or distinguished by a different type, but which the Authorized Version admitted with no such suggestion as to its lack of authority.

11. In the days of King James the current geography and natural history of Bible lands were very imperfect. Little attention had been given to archæology. Egypt and Babylon were less known to the revisers than to us is the heart of Africa or the North Pole. The present century had seen Palestine explored, Jerusalem largely recovered from her ruins, Nineveh and Persepolis unearthed, the faces of the Pharaohs loosed from their cere-

ments, the land which was the scene of Joseph's trials and triumphs quickened into splendor again, and the footprints of Paul traced with such accuracy and care that not even Luke or Timothy seemed more than ourselves to be companions of his travels. The researches and discoveries of the nineteenth century had made the Bible a book more real and living than ever before.

12. Even in the days of the Commonwealth it was matter of complaint that the preachers would display their superior knowledge by differing from the Authorized Version. "The original," they would inform their congregation, "bears it better thus and thus." The consequence was that the weak stumbled and the doubting scoffed. It is needless to say that the habit of criticising the text from the pulpit had not diminished. Dull preachers, who consumed half of their own time and all of their hearers' patience by telling their congregation what the text did not mean, were scarcely more offensive than were the young divines just free from the swaddling clothes of the seminary and the cradle of the class-room, who launched out into the deep of Hebrew and Greek constructions, and floundered in textual criticism, when they might by the mercy of a little modesty have better contented themselves and made proof of their ministry by preaching the gospel. It would be well if by

A.D. 1653.

means of a scholarly revision of the Authorized Version these callow critics found their occupation gone.

For these reasons, and for others besides which need not be recounted, it was argued that a revised version of the English Bible was urgently needed. But there were strong reasons for preserving, as far as possible in any future revision, the idiom and vocabulary of the Authorized Version.

1. Made at the time when the English tongue was best fitted for its task, the Bible of King James was itself an evolution. Many of its happiest phrases were the result of repeated revision. To take only one example of this, how familiar to us is the exclamation of Jesus when he saw Nathanael coming to him, *Behold an Israelite indeed, in whom is no guile* (John 1 : 47). Tyndale rendered the words, *Behold a right Israelite.* The Genevan Bible gave, *Indeed an Israelite.* The Rhemish Version, *An Israelite in very deed.* The Authorized Version alone caught the true rhythm. Dr. Eadie scarcely exaggerates when he says that our version of the Bible has " the fullness of the Bishops' without its frequent literalisms, or its repeated supplements ; it has the graceful vigor of the Geneva, the quiet grandeur of the Great Bible, the clearness of Tyndale's, the harmonies of Coverdale's, and the stately theological vocabulary of the Rheims."

2. No doubt in great measure because they reaped the harvests of two centuries and more of patient research, the revisers succeeded in producing a work of surprising accuracy. It is a Roman Catholic scholar who writes about it, that "Every sentence, every word, every syllable, every letter and point, seem to have been weighed with the nicest exactitude, and expressed, either in the text or margin, with the greatest precision."[1] The substantial progress in biblical scholarship within this century, the examination or actual discovery of the oldest manuscripts of the Greek Testament, made fresh revision imperative. The varieties of readings in the New Testament, reckoned a hundred years ago at about thirty thousand, were now extended to five times that number;[2] but the vast majority of those readings were of no practical importance. The passages in which there are divergencies affecting points of doctrine are very few in number. There is no reason to believe that the faith of Christendom would suffer materially were the labors of the revisers in the reign of James to be left intact. A distinguished member of the New Testament Company, of 1883, sums up the excellencies of the Authorized Version by saying, "It

---

[1] Dr. Alexander Geddes; quoted by Edgar, p. 313.

[2] "Companion to the Revised Version of the New Testament." Alex. Roberts, D. D., p. 7.

is probably the best version ever made for public use. It is not simply a translation but a living reproduction of the original Scriptures in idiomatic English, by men as reverent and devout as they were learned."[1]

3. Published in 1611, our English Bible was associated with some of the greatest events in national and colonial history. The leaders in the civil wars were indebted to its stirring words for many a battle cry, and to its history of the men of whom the world was not worthy, for many an impulse to heroic self-sacrifice. Cromwell exhorted his troops from its pages. Its dramas of ruin and redemption diverted the mind of Milton from the later legend of King Arthur on which he had purposed writing an epic. The very phraseology of the Bible seated itself at the councils of the Commonwealth and forged for the Roundheads the weapons of controversy. When Charles II. recovered his throne, the book had so interwoven itself with all that was best and noblest in the life of the English people that the frivolity of the most frivolous of the Stuarts, and the baseness of the basest of them—his successor, James— were powerless to weaken its hold. It would be almost possible to recover the Bible, were it lost, from the pages of Bunyan's "Pilgrim's Progress," and Baxter's "Saints' Rest." The life of the

---
[1] Roberts, p. 89.

soul was nourished not only by the truths of Scripture, but also by its very language. In the struggles of the English people for their civil rights and religious privileges, as well as in the conflicts of the greatest spiritual leaders; in the Holy War which was waged in the town of Mansoul, and equally in the storming of Leicester and the siege of Londonderry, the Bible of King James played a conspicuous part. It was as dear to the nation as was Magna Charta. Not less was it dear to the hearts of the Puritans and Pilgrims in the New World. Robinson launched the exiles from Holland with a prophecy that fresh light would break forth from God's word, and all colonial history bore witness to the prophetic strain in his famous utterance.

4. Before two hundred years had passed away the Authorized Version had become an inseparable element in our noblest pulpit literature and in our most inspiring sacred song. To it South had been indebted for his virile English; it moved in the majesty of Howe and the melody of Jeremy Taylor; the passion of Baxter caught fire from its rhetoric; the copiousness of Barrow drew its wealth from its pages; there Leighton nourished his unction, and there Thomas Fuller and Joseph Hall their wit. When the eighteenth century quickened the religious life of the country afresh, Wesley found in the gospel his mes-

sage of love, and from the lips of Jeremiah it was that Whitefield caught his impassioned plea, *O earth, earth, earth, hear the word of her Lord.* The prayers of the Puritans were largely expressed in the very language of the Bible, and this continued to be not less true in Boston than it was in London, although unhappily in his preaching the New England divine learned too soon to trust to the subtleties of metaphysics rather than to the *Thus saith the Lord* of the book which made his fathers so brave and so confident. The rhymes of the Bay Psalm-book were uncouth and almost barbarous, but all that was best in them came from the English Bible; while in England herself it was in the truths of the same books, and often in its very language that Doddridge found the inspiration of his polished lines, Watts the evangelical richness of his best hymns, and Charles Wesley the energy and enthusiasm which have crowned him supreme among the sacred singers of England.

The history of the Authorized Version of the English Bible vindicated its claim to remain, even while it added force to the argument for a revision. The great cathedral, which has fallen into disrepair, is far too sacred to the heart of the worshiper to be taken down, although its crumbling buttresses, its shattered carvings, its broken tracery may plead eloquently for careful restoration.

There was no temple in England comparable to her Bible for beauty; about none clustered memories so dear and so inspiring.

The man who in our own age has been called the last of the Puritans, bore his testimony to the power which this book exercised over his whole life, when, in almost his last public utterance, he said: "I would add that not only have we confidence in the word of God in the critic's hand, but we have some of us proof of the word of God in our own daily life, and we would like to bear our own testimony to it. I have tested the word of God in great physical pain. I have had enough of it to be a good and sufficient witness thereto, and there is no pillow for an aching head that is like a promise from the word of God. And I have not been without struggles of another kind than physical; but there is nothing wanted to sustain a man, to put soul into him, but to know that he is in accordance with the mind of Christ; and to take the divine doctrines revealed in that book, and to feed upon them is to make him a giant refreshed with new wine. The book is perfectly wonderful as to its results, when you test them."[1]

Nor was it the least of its virtues that it was the Bible of America as well; and that in the New World as much as in the Old its words were cher-

---

[1] C. H. Spurgeon. Speech for British and Foreign Bible Society, 1890.

ished as an integral part of the nation's heritage. Both England and America might well engage in the pious task of revision, and find therein a new and firmer bond of union. The book was the common possession of both, and both were interested alike in conserving its associations, and in making it a still more faithful reflection of the mind of the Spirit.

VIII.

THE ENGLISH OF THE VERSIONS.

"When viewed simply in its literary aspect, the history of the growth of the Authorized Text involves a more comprehensive and subtle criticism, and is therefore filled with a deeper interest than any similar history."

—*Westcott, History of the English Bible.*

CHAPTER VIII.

THE ENGLISH OF THE VERSIONS.

THE history of the English Bible is substantially the history of the English tongue. From 1380, when Wycliffe completed the English New Testament, to 1611, when the Authorized Version appeared, our language was passing through various stages of change and progress. At first a tongue almost unintelligible to us to-day, it grew into a tongue differing from our own scarcely at all. A glance at some of the changes which our English Bible registers will now be in place. We must estimate at their true worth the successive transitions which consummated in the book of which Canon Liddon said: "When we take up the Bible we enter a splendid temple built not out of stone and marble, but with human words." [A. D. 1380.]

John Purvey was an immediate follower of John Wycliffe. Eight years only passed after Wycliffe published his translation, before Purvey published his revision of it. Yet even in that short time (1380–1388) the language was altering, both in the words themselves, and in their arrangement. A comparison of the two ren- [A. D. 1388.]

derings will suffice to illustrate this. We take it from the history of Joseph:[1]

WYCLIFFE AND HEREFORD, 1380.	PURVEY'S REVISION, 1388.
Gen. 41 : 43. *And made him steye upon his secound chaar, crying a bedel, that alle men shoulden bifore him knele, and they shoulden wite hym to be prouest to all the loond of Egypte.*	Gen. 41 : 43. *And Faroa made Joseph to stie on his secound chare, while a bidele criede that alle men schulden kneele bifore hym, and schulden knowe that he was souereyn of all the lond of Egypt.*

The plural ending *en* in nouns was more common then than now, and it is interesting to note that still more commonly it was used in the plurals of verbs. Thus we read in Purvey's Version: *The disciplis zeden and didden as Jesus commanded hem, and thei brouzten an asse, and the fole, and leiden her clothis on him, and maden hym sitte above* (Matt. 21 : 6, 7).

The way in which prepositions are used seems strange to us now, although in some parts of England traces of the same usage linger yet. *In the bigynnynge was the word, and the word was at God* (John 1 : 1). *In that tyme ihesus wente bi cornes in the Saboth dai* (Mark 2 : 23). The verbs derived from adjectives are often so expressive that we regret their loss in our language to-day. *Eche that enhauncith hym schall be* lowed, *and he that* mekith *hym schall be* hized (Luke 14 : 11). Rarely

---

[1] For numerous references in this chapter I am indebted to Dr. Edgar's "Bibles of England."

PORTION OF WYCLIFFE'S BIBLE.
Page 132.

is the language of Wycliffe or Purvey lacking in force, that one quality which is more likely to diminish than to increase with the advance of culture. There is, for example, a picture in one word when we read that, in the miracle on the lake of Galilee, the devils went out from the man and entered into the swine, and *with a birre the flok wente headlynge into the pool* (Luke 8 : 33), and when we are told that being called by Jesus, Bartimeus *castid aweie his cloth, and skeppid, and cam*. There is more force than elegance in the early rendering of Jude 19 : *Beestli men, not havynge Spirit*, instead of *sensual, having not the Spirit*. Perhaps it is the graphic strength of Wycliffe's Bible that more than anything else makes it so intelligible still. Words that have passed away, being dead yet speak. Especially in the North of England, where our language still carries a force which we search for in vain in the softer South, is this true. Not many years ago, when the experiment of reading Wycliffe's translation aloud was tried in Yorkshire, there was hardly a word or an expression which seemed at all peculiar.[1]

2. But it is in Tyndale's translation that we find most of the strength, as well as most of the sweetness of our Authorized Version. To the laws of spelling he was as

A. D. 1525-6.

---

[1] "Christian Annotator," Vol. III., p. 58; quoted by Eadie, Vol. I., p. 78.

indifferent as were his contemporaries. He was by no means confined to one way only for each word that he used. But he sinned in the best of company, and it is conceivable that in our own day the next reform in spelling may leave us to the full as much license as was taken by the writers of the sixteenth century. Turning to more important matters, however, we may notice a few of the characteristics by virtue of which Tyndale's Version won its high place in English literature. There is a graphic simplicity about it which captures the ear at once. *There were many comers and goers, that they had no leisure so moche as to eat* (Mark 6 : 31), gives us at a stroke the restless crowd beside the lake; *All the city was on a roore* (Acts 19 : 29), rouses for us the voices of the craftsmen of Ephesus; the tempestuous wind called Euroclydon seems to blow harder when depicted as *a flawe of wynde out of the north-easte* (Acts 27 : 14); and the Spirit searching even *the deep things of God*, fails to carry the force of *the bottome of Goddes secretes* (1 Cor. 2 : 10). Tyndale's own experience with the ecclesiastical leaders of his day may have helped him to point his pen with such phrases as, *He is pufte up and knoweth nothinge, but wasteth his braynes about questions and stryfe of words;* and *If eny of you lacke wysdom, let him axe of God which geveth to all men indifferentlie, and casteth no man in the teth.* One of his translations: *Likewis, also the prelates mocking him*, so plainly betrayed the feeling of the exile banished by the bishops that it was changed in the next and revised edition.[1] The music of Tyndale's translation with equal ease rises to the stately majesty of a march, or falls to the homelike sweetness of a mother's lullaby. The arrangement of words in such a sentence as *Hosanna, blessed is he that in the name of the Lorde cometh Kynge of Israel*, is in itself triumphal. The alliteration in *the halte which was healed helde Peter* (Acts 3: 11), impresses the scene on our memories; we see the hungry multitude awaiting Christ's miracle with the loaves as they *sate down here a row and there a rowe, by hundreds and fifties;* there is truth as well as beauty in declaring that *an avaricious man is the thraldome of idolatrie* (Eph. 5:5); we catch with all its wonderful emphasis Paul's memorable cry in *Alas! I, caitiff man, who shall deliver me from my caitiff body* (Rom. 7:24); and no one who has once heard it can ever lose the pathos of our Lord's tone in the expression: *That lost child*, which Tyndale gives us instead of *that son of perdition*, to which we are more used.

3. Coverdale was chiefly indebted to Tyndale, but he also used Dutch and Latin translations of the Old Testament, and the influence of Luther is very apparent. To origi-

A.D. 1535-9.

---

[1] Eadie, Vol. I., p. 155.

nality he made no pretense. "Lowly and faithfully," says he, in his dedication to the king, "have I followed mine interpreters, and that under correction." There are occasionally renderings which by their quaintness attract our attention; but they are rarely original, and as a rule, may be traced to the Vulgate, if they are not found in Luther's translation. Such for instance, are *O! who will geve my head waters ynough*, for "Oh that my head were waters" (Jer. 9 : 1); *A still soft hissing*, for "a still small voice"; and *hath comprehended all the earth of the world in thie fingers*, for "the dust of the earth in a measure." The rendering of Jer. 8 : 22 : "There is no treacle in Galaad," transferred to the Bishops' Bible, won for it the name of The Treacle Bible, although Coverdale was responsible for the translation. Better known, although not so pleasant in its associations, is his unfortunate rendering of the words so dear to us in our Authorized Version: "Thou shalt not be afraid for the terror by night (Ps. 91 : 5)," which Coverdale turns into: *Thou shalt not nede to be afrayed for eny bugges by night.* Much happier is his translation of Isaiah 51 : 20: *Thy sons have fainted, they lie at the head of all the streets as a taken venyson.* A captured deer is singularly helpless, and Coverdale's choice of a word in this instance is remarkably graphic. The Scottish dialect of to-day helps us to understand how the dove *bare an olive branch in hir nebb* (Gen. 8 : 11); but we have lost entirely that special use of a very expressive word which could excuse Job's exclamation: *What manner of felowe is the Almightie, that we should serve him?* (Job 21 : 15). The translator shows that he can change an indifferent word for a better, when for *Thou sendest gracious rayne upon thine inheritance, and refreshest it when it is dry, that thy beastes may dwell therein*, was substituted "thy congregation."

4. The Genevan Bible, which in the Old Testament remained in its first version, was in the New Testament successively published in 1557 and 1560, at Geneva, and in London in 1576, with many changes introduced by Lawrence Tomson. The city of their exile was the city of two of the most accomplished scholars of their time, and we are not surprised that the translators were moved "with one assent to requeste two off their brethern, to witt, Calvin and Beza eftsounes to peruse the same, notwithstandynge their former trauells."[1] It was the Latin New Testament of Beza which most powerfully influenced the Genevan Version. But there were many eminent men about the same time occupied in the work of Bible translation. The scholarly air must have been congenial to the task, and Europe never saw a theocracy so nearly established as in

A. D. 1557-60.

---
[1] Edgar, p. 166.

those memorable years in the history of the bright little city of Geneva. The title by which the Genevan Bible is popularly known, "The Breeches Bible," comes from the rendering of the last clause of Gen. 3:7: *They sewed figge leaves together, and made themselves breeches.* But notwithstanding occasional archaisms, the Genevan Version is marked by refined diction. It gave to us many of the "words and phrases, and entire sentences which have ever since been retained in the English Bibles of the Protestant Churches," and many more "made their first appearance in a crude and unfinished form," which afterward more polished, took their place in the Authorized Version.[2]

The old-fashioned word "dame," which lingers yet in Eton School, is found in Hagar's answer to the angel, *I flee from my dame Sarai* (Gen. 16:8). As was fitting in the city of Calvin, the shout, "Good lucke, good lucke," which hails the crowning of the second temple in Coverdale's Version, becomes with the Genevans, *Grace, grace.* "Patron" has fallen into disuse with us, although it lingered long in Holland and lingers still in Italy; but in the first Genevan New Testament we read: *The under captayne believed the governor and* the patron *of the ship better than those things which were spoken of Paul* (Acts

---
[2] Edgar, p. 170.

27 : 11). To the Genevan translators we owe the rhythm in the assurance: *She hath received of the Lord's hand double for all her sins.* The great words of Job: *For I am sure that my Redeemer liveth, and he shall stand the last on the earth* (Job 19 : 25), is nearer to the original than are earlier renderings. The Authorized Version did well to retain the happy paraphrase in Acts 20 : 24, *None of these things move me*, and from Geneva also came the noble rendering of a critical passage: *The cup of blessing which we bless, is it not the communion of the blood of Christ? The bread which we break, is it not the communion of the body of Christ?* (1 Cor. 10 : 16.)

5. If Coverdale was indebted to Tyndale, the Bishops' Bible was even more indebted to Coverdale. It differed indeed from former versions and anticipated the Authorized Version in being the work of many rather than of one. But the influence of Coverdale and of the Great Bible, which was little more than an amendment of it, is easily traced in many of the books of the Bishops' Bible. In others again it is evident that they appropriate the renderings of the Genevans. The English of the Bishops' Bible is not free from the affectations of that age, but occasionally it becomes graphic and (although not so often) melodious. *He that is suretie for a stranger shall smart for it* (Prov. 11 : 15), has

A. D. 1568.

passed into a "current proverb." There is point in, *A housewifely woman is a crown unto her husband* (Prov. 12 : 4). The Authorized Version altered only slightly the vivid rendering from Nahum's burden of Nineveh: *The rattling of wheels, the prancing of horses, and the jumping of chariots* (Nahum 3 : 2). The translation, *Is there no treacle in Galaad?* which, as we have seen, gave to the Bishops' Bible the nickname of the Treacle Bible, is not indeed as touching as our own : *Is there no balm in Gilead?* but at the time when it was made it was probably quite as accurate. We have to thank the Bishops' Bible for such renderings as : *Right and light shall be with thee, and with every one that is godly in thee* (Deut. 33 : 8); and, *Which rejoice exceedingly and are glad when they can find the grave* (Job 3 : 22); and for a form which is as familiar in our ears as it is urgent on our consciences, *Rend your hearts and not your garments* (Joel 2 : 13).

A. D. 1607-11. 6. The Authorized Version was not only more faithful to the original than any which had appeared before it, but it was also a finer piece of English. Never before had our English tongue been so worthy as it was at just that time to do this work ; and it may confidently be affirmed that it has never been so worthy since. With the exception of the Roman Catholic version, each successive rendering of our English

Bible had registered a higher mark than its predecessor. Preserving what was best, and amending what was not satisfactory, our translators had moved on triumphantly through a formative period in the history of our language. When our Authorized Version appeared, it appeared as the survival of the fittest in the choice of words and in the cast of sentences. Such is the genius of the Authorized Version that we find ourselves in hearty accord with the poet Rogers, when he says: "Oh, the exquisite English of the Bible! I often feel as if the translators as well as the original writers must have been inspired."

All previous versions were laid under contribution. No prejudice against Papist or Puritan was suffered to debar Rhemish or Genevan; and if the translators of King James' Version rarely go back of the text of the Bishops' Bible to an earlier English rendering,[1] this may be because this version was itself the harvest of the labors of its predecessors. How truly our English Bible is a growth will be seen if we trace the process of development through which a single verse passed before, like a fine piece of pottery, it had reached perfection. The words of Jesus, "Settle it therefore in your hearts not to meditate before what ye shall answer" (Luke 21 : 14), read better in this their final form than the Genevan: *Lay it by*,

---
[1] Westcott, p. 338.

therefore, in your hearts, that ye premeditate not; as the Genevan was an improvement upon the Great Bible and the Bishops' Bible: *Be at a sure point in your hearts not to study before;* and all of them are preferable to Tyndale: *Let it stick, therefore, fast in your hearts not once to study before what he shall answer.*[1] Occasionally, but not often, the older versions are better than the new. "Took up our carriages" (Acts 21 : 15) is better than *trussed up our fardels*, of the Genevan; and yet is inferior to *took up our burdens* as the Bishops' rendered the words of Luke; while Tyndale's, *made ourselves ready*, is perhaps not so close, but in all other points it is the happiest rendering of any of them.

A whole chapter might be devoted to the subject of printers' errors in various editions of the English Bible; but no other purpose would be served by it than to entertain the reader with illustrations of the curiosities of literature. In the edition of the Authorized Bible, published in 1631, the omission of the word *not* completely reversed the meaning of the seventh commandment, and probably the printer got his deserts when he was fined three hundred pounds for his blunder. A similar oversight mars many other Bibles, although never in so important a passage. *Him that taketh away thy cloke, forbid to take thy coat also* (Luke

---

[1] Edgar, p. 312.

6 : 29), is a command easier to obey than the original; and such misprints as *vinegar* for "vineyard," *ate her* for "hate her," *eyes* for "ears," *covereth* for "converted," are curious examples taken from a sheaf of errors in the printers' chapter of accidents. The patent to print Bibles exclusively was not, perhaps, ill bestowed upon the Barkers, whose work was generally well done; but certainly never was monopoly more shamefully abused than by a Mrs. Anderson, who, from 1676 to 1711, was the licensed printer of Bibles for Scotland. Her opponents scored a point against her when they extracted the following piece of confused type-setting from one of her Bibles printed in 1705: "whyshoulditbethougtathingincredible w^t you, y^t God should raise the dead?"[1] No more powerful argument could be brought than is furnished by this comedy of errors for leaving with a nation the right to print and publish the book which is its peculiar treasure. The printers' monopoly was destined to follow the monopolies of churches and kings. The people may be trusted to see to it that no dishonor is done to the noblest achievement in their literature, and that the butter is *brought forth in a lordly dish* (Judges 5 : 25). The history of the English Bible from the time of Wycliffe to our own day is full of proof that the people are more conservative than the scholars,

---
[1] Edgar, p. 298.

and will not lightly suffer anything which savors of what they deem a tampering with the sacred text. Whatever may be the future of Bible revision, no changes in the English of our translations can affect the place which the Authorized Version holds in our literature, and certainly never was what Dante so happily calls "the sieve for noble words" used to higher advantage.

IX.

THE REVISED VERSION.

"To whom was it ever imputed for a fault (by such as were wise,) to go over that which he hath done, and to amend it when he saw cause? If we will be sons of the truth, we must consider what it speaketh, and trample upon our own credit, yea, and upon other men's too, if either be any way an hindrance to it."—*Preface to King James' Bible.*

CHAPTER IX.

THE REVISED VERSION.

On the 10th of February, 1870, the Upper House of the Convocation of Canterbury, adopted a resolution looking toward revision, which ran thus:

"That a committee of both Houses be appointed to report upon the desirableness of a Revision of the Authorized Version of the Old and New Testaments, whether by marginal notes or otherwise, in those passages where plain and clear errors, whether in the Hebrew or Greek text originally adopted by the translators, or in the translation made from the same, shall on due investigation be found to exist."

The resolution was moved by Dr. Wilberforce, bishop of Winchester, and seconded by Dr. Ellicott, bishop of Gloucester and Bristol. That these men should have been willing to give their sanction to such a movement spoke well for its ultimate success. Wilberforce inherited a great name, and had added fresh lustre to it. Although he failed to carry on the evangelical succession of which his father, by his writings and example was a foremost ornament, he yet possessed not a little of his father's adroitness and very much of his father's persuasive eloquence. Dr. Ellicott, in his turn, was in the front ranks of New Testament exegetes, so that if the name of Wilberforce was likely to win popular approval for the proposal, that of his companion was, at all events, sure to command for it the respect of all scholarly men.

Three months after the passing of this resolution the two Houses of Convocation, with slight dissent, decided that a revision ought to be undertaken. The report in which this conviction was embodied proposed that Convocation, "should nominate a body of its own members to undertake the work of revision, who shall be at liberty to invite the co-operation of any, eminent for scholarship, to whatever nation or religious body they may belong." It is obvious at once that a revision of the English Bible in a country such as England must originate with the Established Church if it is to attain to the dignity of a national achievement. The English people would be satisfied with no other. "The Church of England is the mother of the Authorized Version, and has an undoubted right to take the lead in any movement for an improvement of the same. She still represents the largest membership, the strongest institutions, the richest literature, among those ecclesiastical organizations which have sprung from the common English stock. She would never accept a revision made by any other denomination. She has all the necessary qualifications of learning and piety to produce without foreign aid as good a version for our age as King James' revisers produced for their age."[1]

But the day has passed in which the English-speaking nations would be satisfied with a Bible carrying the imprimatur of any one section of the universal church. There is no longer a church established by law controlling all the countries in which the English Bible is read, and the threat which King James I. flung at the dissenters, "I will make them conform themselves, or else I will harry them out of the land, or else I will just hang them, that is all," if uttered by the sovereign to-day might cost him his head, and would certainly cost him his throne. The Committee of Convocation resolved to invite about forty biblical scholars, chosen from the Church of England and other churches, to share their labors. With very few exceptions—Cardinal Newman was one of these—the scholars who were invited accepted. The Episcopalians, as was naturally to be expected, had the majority on the Committee of Revision when it first met, and a bishop presided over both the Old and New Testament companies. In 1880 the number of revisers amounted to fifty-two, and of these, thirty-six were Episcopalians equally divided between the two companies, while

---

[1] Roberts p. 91.

the remainder were Presbyterians, Congregationalists, Baptists, and Methodists, including one Unitarian. The Baptist members of the Committee were Dr. Benjamin Davies, whose profound learning and childlike piety made him the object of mingled reverence and love with his students of Regents' Park College, London; Dr. Gotch, his life-long friend, who was at this time president of the Baptist College, Bristol; and Dr. Joseph Angus, who by his loyalty to our principles, attainments, and statesmanlike sagacity, was the accepted representative of the denomination. After a brief religious service in the chapel of King Henry VII., Westminster Abbey, the committee began its work on the 22nd of June, 1870. The New Testament company met in the Jerusalem Chamber, a large hall in the Westminster Deanery, which was itself rich in historical memories.[1] Here, in the days which preceded the Reformation, the abbot and his friends gathered for social intercourse. Before the fire burning in the hearth—the fireplace in the room was one of the earliest fitted for burning sea-coal—King Henry IV. died. Disappointed in his hope to make a pilgrimage to the Holy Land, he found some solace in the name of the room

"Bear me to that chamber; there I'll lie:
In that Jerusalem shall Harry die."[2]

---

[1] See paragraph at the end of this chapter.
[2] Shakespeare "Henry IV."

THE REVISED VERSION. 151

The Scripture tapestries which hang from the walls looked down more than two hundred years later on the famous Westminster assembly of divines, who met here, as Thomas Fuller says, "for the building of Zion." Now after a lapse of two hundred and thirty years, the world was ready for this more conspicuous spectacle, this reunion of Christendom on the only basis on which that reunion will ever be possible. The preface to the Revised Version is dated from the Jerusalem Chamber—the place of which Henry Ward Beecher said: "No room has greater interest for me, unless it be the 'Upper Room'"—and will for all time be the noblest memory associated with its walls. When the two companies met simultaneously, the Old Testament company assembled in the Chapter Library of the Deanery; at other times it also gathered in the Jerusalem Chamber.

The New Testament Company had completed the first revision in about six years; two years more were spent in a second revision, and only after two years and a half had passed were all the details reserved for final discussion settled, so that the work could be issued from the press. The Old Testament revision required fourteen years. From the preface to the New Version we learn that it was "completed in eighty-five sessions, ending on June 20, 1884; and it occupied seven hundred and ninety-two days. The greater part of the sessions were for ten days each; and each day the company generally sat for six hours."

The Committee had not been long at work before the claims of America to a share in this enterprise were recognized. By the request of Bishop Ellicott, Dr. Angus, who visited the United States in 1870, conferred with some American scholars, and at his suggestion they drew up a plan of co-operation, and suggested a list of names, both of which, substantially, were approved by the English Companies. "In view of the great distance, it was deemed best to organize a separate Committee, that should fairly represent the biblical scholarship of the leading churches and literary institutions of the United States. Such a Committee, consisting of about thirty members, was formed in 1871, and entered upon active work in October, 1872, when the first revision of the synoptical Gospels was received. It was likewise divided into two Companies, which met every month (except in July and August) in the Bible House at New York,—but without any connection with the American Bible Society,—and co-operated with their English brethren on the same principles and with the intention of bringing out one and the same revision for both countries. Ex-President Dr. Woolsey, of New Haven, acted as permanent chairman of the New Testament Company; Dr. Green, professor in Princeton, as chairman of the Old Testament Company. The two Committees exchanged the results of their labors in confidential communications."[1]

In these committees the names of Dr. T. J. Conant and Dr. Howard Osgood, in the Old Testament Committee; and of Dr. Horatio B. Hackett and Dr. Asahel C. Kendrick, in the New Testament Committee, did honor to the scholarship of our Baptist institutions of learning.

That there should be certain difficulties in fusing the labors of two bodies so far separated as were the English and American Companies was inevitable. It was only in July, 1875, that a plan was matured for the consolidation of the international forces. Dr. Schaff, himself the president of the American Committee, describes it thus: "The English revisers promise to send confidentially their revision in its various stages to the American revisers, to take all the American suggestions into special consideration before the conclusion of their labors, to furnish them, before publication, with copies of the revision in its final form, and to allow them to present in an appendix to the revised Scriptures, all the remaining differences of reading and rendering of importance which the English Committee should decline to adopt; while, on the other hand, the American revisers pledge themselves to give their moral

---
[1] Roberts, pp. 92, 93.

support to the Authorized editions of the University Presses, with a view to their freest circulation within the United States, and not to issue an edition of their own for a term of fourteen years."[1] Although the best part of the American labor is incorporated in the book itself, yet the appendix is a substantial memorial of independent scholarship, and it is safe to anticipate that many of the changes which it advocates will ultimately find their way into the margins of our Bible, and thence in turn into the text itself. Where, however, the American renderings affect the idioms of our language, it is questionable whether in their anxiety to be faithful to the original and consistent with the principles of translation which they had laid down for themselves, the revisers have not too often clouded the well of pure English undefiled which is so dear to all lovers of our tongue. One point more needs to be noticed here. "At an early stage in our labors," we read in the New Testament Preface, "we entered into an agreement with the universities of Oxford and Cambridge for the conveyance to them of our copyright in the work. This arrangement provided for the necessary expenses of the undertaking; and procured for the Revised Version the advantage of being published by bodies long con-

---

[1] "A companion to the Greek Testament and the English Version," Philip Schaff, D. D., pp. 66, 400, 401.

nected with the publication of the Authorized Version." The fact that the university publishers met the expenses of the English Committee, and received in return the copyright of the Revised Version, while extremely honorable to the devotion and unselfishness of the Committee, left their American colleagues without means to pay the cost of their labor, and the English printers no guarantee as to the sale of the work in this country. The funds for the necessary expenses of the American revisers were contributed by private donors; and as to the profit of the sale of the version in America, while the moral support, as we have seen, of those who engaged in the enterprise was cast on the side of the agents of the English publishers in this country, it was impossible to do more than this. "The New Version stands precisely on the same footing with the old version as to copyright: it is protected by law in England, it is free in America."

On both sides of the sea the ripest scholarship of our century was freely given to this great work. A harvest to the publishers, there was not even a scanty gleaning for those who toiled under the burden and heat of the day. The tribute which the Preface pays to the American committee we may well adopt in reference to each body of the revisers. "We gratefully acknowledge their care, vigilance, and accuracy, and we humbly pray that their labors, thus happily united, may be permitted to bear a blessing to both countries, and to all English-speaking people throughout the world."

For such a revision of the Scripture the time was certainly ripe. Unlike the plan adopted by the translators of the Authorized Version, the revisers did not now divide the books among sub-committees, "but each company assumed its whole share, thus securing greater uniformity and consistency"; for one of the aims of the new version was to produce a work distinguished by greater consistency in the principle of translation than is to be found in the older book. Five classes of alterations are mentioned in the Preface to the New Testament, namely: Such as are positively required by change of reading in the Greek text; such as are necessitated because the Authorized Version appeared to be incorrect, or to have chosen the less probable of two possible renderings; alterations of obscure or ambiguous renderings; alterations where the Authorized Version was inconsistent with itself; and such as were rendered necessary *by consequence*—that is, arising out of changes already made, though not in themselves required by the general rule of faithfulness.[1]

The advance in scholarship, as well as in dis-

---

[1] "Preface to the New Testament," Revised Version.

covery, during the nineteenth century seemed to demand that before its close a careful revision of our English Bible should be made. For a hundred years or more new translations of the whole Bible, or of important parts of it, had been appearing. Campbell and MacKnight and Newcome did the work before the eighteenth century had passed away; during the first half of our century, Noah Webster and Nathan Hale in America, and in England Samuel Sharpe and many others had given practical expression by their independent versions to the sense of dissatisfaction with the Authorized Version.[1] From 1850 onward, it seemed as though the scholars who were to do the work of revision were already gathering in the field. Five Anglican clergymen published in 1857 the Gospel of John and the Pauline Epistles, and of these, Dean Alford and Bishop Ellicott were afterward chosen among the revisers, although Alford's death (January, 1871), closed his arduous and successful labors as a New Testament exegete. Four English scholars, Gotch, Davies, Jacob, and S. G. Green—three of them Baptists—prepared a Revised English Bible, much of which must have anticipated the action of Convocation. "The American Bible Union, a Baptist organization in America, spent for nearly twenty years a vast amount of money, zeal, and labor on an Improved

---

[1] Schaff, p. 366.

Version, and published the New Testament in full and the Old Testament in part, with learned comments, the best of them by Dr. Conant, on Job, Psalms, and Proverbs."[1] At no previous time had the text of the New Testament been so ready for translation, and never before had the lands of the Bible been so well understood.

The Preface to the Revised Version describes with sufficient fullness the rules which the companies adopted. If they erred at all, they certainly erred on the side of caution. The Episcopal Church was true to its traditional reputation for conservatism. Only very occasionally were changes made which seriously affected the traditional text. The concluding clause of the Lord's Prayer was omitted from the Gospel by Matthew, but it was given a place in the margin. The last twelve verses of the Gospel by Mark were preserved, although they were now separated by a distinct space from the early part of the chapter, and a marginal note left their genuineness in doubt. Important doctrinal teaching was affected by the new version of such passages as 2 Tim. 3 : 16 and 2 Tim. 2 : 26. In the few instances in which the Authorized Version left the sense obscure—such as Heb. 4 : 8—a simple change cleared the text up at once. In the Old Testament, the surprise was not that so much, but that so little had

---

[1] Schaff, p. 367.

to be altered. The revisers have frequently given expression to their admiration for the scholarship of the translators who met at the bidding of King James. As a summary, it may be said that out of the seven hundred and ninety-one thousand four hundred and forty-four words composing the Revised Bible, seven hundred and twenty-one thousand six hundred and seventy-one are the same as are found in the old version. Only nine per cent.—seventy thousand seven hundred and seventy-two—have been changed; while sixty-five thousand five hundred and eight have been excluded.

The New Testament was ready for publication early in 1881. On the 17th of May, Bishop Ellicott, who had been associated with Bishop Wilberforce eleven years before in moving Convocation to action, laid the first copy of the Revised New Testament before that body, and proceeded to give a brief history of the work which was now completed. Already a million copies had been called for in England and America. Within a few days of its publication nearly three hundred and sixty-five thousand copies of the Clarendon Press edition had been sold in New York. Other editions rapidly appeared. Two daily papers in Chicago had the book telegraphed to them from New York, and gave it complete in their columns as soon as possible after publication. It is estimated that less than a year had passed before three million copies had been bought in Great Britain and America. The entire Bible was published on the 19th of May, 1885, and if the excitement attending the publication of the New Testament was absent on this occasion, the feeling was deeper and more serious, and the general judgment on the book was more satisfactory. For, as must always be recognized in any history of the English Bible, during the four years which passed since the Revised Version of the New Testament appeared, it had gone through a furnace of criticism. Although the proportion of changes in the new version is not large, yet it is sufficient to warrant Dr. Mombert's opinion: "The term revision seems to have been construed very liberally; for strictly speaking the Revised Version is a new translation on the basis of the Authorized Version."[1] Had the revision stopped with the New Testament these words would have been especially true. Of necessity the Old Testament was less changed. The scholarship of the church had concerned itself during the first part of the nineteenth century with Greek rather than with Hebrew. The controversies now waging in England and America over the Old Testament Scriptures had not then assumed such importance. While there were many passages in the Authorized Version of the

---
[1] Mombert, p. 464.

Old Testament which were obscure, and some which were even unintelligible, yet on the whole there was less scope for delicate and discerning scholarship in dealing with it, than there was in revising the New Testament. Possibly the unfavorable reception given to many of the revised readings of the New Testament company made their brethren of the Old Testament company more conservative. However this may have been, it is certain that the appearance of the complete Bible in the Revised Version was not assailed by the opposition which greeted the New Testament alone.

On a calm examination it was found that there were very few changes which seriously affected the doctrinal teaching of familiar verses. Here and there indeed, a text was so entirely altered that the preacher saw with reluctance his favorite sermon wrecked almost before its voyage began, and had no alternative but to abandon his discourse, unless he was prepared to sail under false colors. The revision of the Scriptures has drawn attention afresh to the importance of exegesis, and is fast making it impossible for even the most unscrupulous pulpit orator to treat his Bible as no other professional man, with an atom of self-respect, would dare treat his text-books.

The fiercest onslaught upon the text of the Revised Version was made by Dr. Burgon, dean of

Chichester, a man of genuine if somewhat unequal scholarship, but of a temper so willful and impetuous that it virtually unfitted him for controversy. Twelve years before the new version appeared, Dean Burgon had published an elaborate defense of the genuineness of the last twelve verses of Mark. He now hastened into the field with three articles in the Quarterly Review, which were afterward issued in one volume under the title of "The Revision Revised," and in which, after criticising the English of the version as "hopelessly at fault,"—an opinion in which he was supported by so eminent a judge as Matthew Arnold,—he proceeded to consider at length the systematic depravation of the underlying Greek as nothing else but "a poisoning of the 'River of Life' at its sacred source." Men of cooler judgment, although possibly of inferior scholarship, while not prepared to go to such lengths as Dean Burgon, have come to the conclusion that the revisers may have adopted too narrow a conception of what a translation should be. They have inquired whether it is safe to lay so much stress on the shades of meaning in words and tenses, or the precise force of particles, in translating the language of writers who were not themselves as a rule practised grammarians. They have pointed to passages in the Authorized Version where a happy paraphrase has seemed to do justice to the mind of the spirit as a literal translation would not.[1] Such questions, however, belong to the critic rather than to the general reader. The great majority of the people to whom the Bible was dear, hailed the Revised Version with pleasure; bought it when it appeared with eagerness; glanced over its pages with interest; and then returned to the Authorized Version, grateful that they had been deprived of so small a portion of their household treasure. The men who had inherited the Puritan love for the very letter of the Scriptures were many of them indignant at proposed changes which would rob them of texts familiar in their mouths as household words. "We did not need," Mr. Spurgeon wrote, in noticing the Revised Old Testament, "a blunder Bible to complete the series of eccentric Scriptures. However, good has come out of evil; The old Authorized Version sits secure upon its throne. There is none like it; nor is there likely to be." Dean Burgon warned the Canadian Episcopal Synod against sanctioning "the grossest blunder of the age." Mr. Gladstone wrote to the fiery dean in terms more politic, certainly, but still adverse to the English of the new version; and the devout Lord Iddersleigh, himself as competent a scholar as Mr. Gladstone, was of opinion that "the travesty of the whole text of the Scripture destroys far more than it can possibly give in re-

A. D. 1886.

---

[1] Mombert, p. 17. See also Schaff's "Companion, etc.," p. 46.

turn." Enthusiastic admirers of the splendid prose of the Elizabethan era sarcastically characterized the language of the revision as "Fifth Form English," and Dr. A. K. H. Boyd, as a man of delicately attuned ear, found it "not irritating but infuriating." That the rhythm of the Authorized Version had often been sacrificed on the altar of grammatical accuracy was recognized by Dr. Howard Crosby, and perhaps other of the revisers, and Mr. John Bright—who in common with his friend, Mr. Gladstone, preferred such archaic forms as "Our Father *which* art in heaven," to "who art in heaven,"—expressed the general feeling in reference to the English of the new version when he said: "I do not think the revisers understood English as well as the translators of the Authorized Version, however much better they may have understood Greek." In two successive volumes, Mr. G. Washington Moon, who had constituted himself the guardian of the Queen's English, exposed the reviser's violations of the laws of language with a minuteness which made his readers grateful that he had not lived two centuries and a half earlier, to break a lance with the English of the King James' Company. He probably gave utterance to a growing conviction when he refused to see in the new version anything more than an experiment, which the revisers issued preliminary to one that would in due time appear with the sanc-

THE REVISED VERSION. 165

tion of royal and ecclesiastical authority. What is certain, is that although the work was begun at the instigation of Convocation, the Revised Version has not as yet taken the place of the Authorized Version in the services of the Established Church of England. It has not received the sanction of the great Bible Societies. With few exceptions, it has not found its way into the pulpits of our churches, and these exceptions are not of such weight as to warrant the confident prediction of Dr. Schaff that the old version is "now doomed to a peaceful and honorable burial."[1] There is still too much love for the noblest language used in the holiest services, too much inherent and often unconscious delight in stately and melodious rhetoric, as well as too much attachment to the book which, more than any other, is associated with all that is most heroic in our history and most sacred in our experience, for such a forecast as this to be verified. No doubt the Revised Version appeared at the most favorable time for the claim of textual accuracy, but it appeared also in an evil time for the claims of good English. It was no fault of the revisers that troopers and traders in the reign of King James used language richer and more musical than is used by ministers of religion and members of Parliament in the reign of Queen Victoria. The golden era of our tongue had passed away

---
[1] Schaff, p. 370.

long before the companies met in the Jerusalem Chamber.

But it must always remain a matter for regret that a profound acquaintance with the dead languages was not accompanied in the case of the revisers by an adequate reverence for the living tongue with which they were dealing.

There were masters of English still with us when the revision was making who, not less than the revisers themselves, loved the Bible; who with intelligence equal to theirs, pored over its pages, and whose exquisite appreciation of melody might have preserved without any sacrifice of textual accuracy, "the happy terms of expression, the music of the cadences, the felicities of the rhythm of the Authorized Version." Tennyson, the most melodious of the Victorian poets, was himself a competent Greek scholar; Matthew Arnold, who had no superior in clear and forcible English, had made studies in the Old Testament; John Bright was the foremost orator of his time, and scarcely a week passed in which in his home circle the Bible, read aloud with his noble emphasis, did not receive a new tribute of exposition; while the greatest prose writer of the century, John Ruskin, had been trained from his mother's knee in passionate devotion to the language of the Scriptures. It may fairly be questioned whether ever again will so many masters of our tongue be

Entrance to the Jerusalem Chamber, Westminster Abbey.

Page 167.

available for such a service as these men, and others who might be named, could have rendered to the revisers. But the opportunity was lost, and because of its loss the whole English-speaking world is the poorer to-day. The years which have now passed since the Revised Version appeared have virtually settled its place in the history of the English Bible. Already there are indications that the revision may itself need to be revised, nor does there seem to be any good reason why, with our increasing knowledge of the lands and languages of the Bible, another new revision shall not come in due time. Meanwhile the lover of his Bible should be the first to acknowledge the great debt which he owes to the men who in England and America, working harmoniously together for nearly fifteen years, gave to us the most valuable commentary upon the Scriptures that has ever been published. The Revised Version may never supersede the Authorized, but it has already added immensely to our knowledge of the book to which alike the companies in the seventeenth and the nineteenth centuries consecrated so much of their learning and of their lives.

So much interest attaches to the *Jerusalem Chamber*, the room in which the work of the revisers was carried on, that the following information, for which I am indebted to H. Burke Downing, Esq., F. R. I. B. A., will be welcome to the reader: "The Jerusalem Chamber is an apartment or council chamber adjoining the grand dining hall of the abbots' palace, now the deanery of Westminster, which after the fashion of the age in which it was built, is arranged around an irregular quadrangle that goes by the name of Cheyney Gate Manor. Stanley, in his 'Memorials of Westminster Abbey,' says of it that already 'even in the middle ages it had become historical.' In the time of Henry IV. it was still but a private apartment, the withdrawing room or guest chamber of the abbot—opening on one hand into the abbot's refectory, on the other into his yard or garden—just rebuilt by Nicholas Lillington, and deriving the name of 'Jerusalem,' probably from the tapestries or pictures of the history of Jerusalem, as the Antioch Chamber in the palace of Westminster was so called from pictures representing the siege of Antioch."

X.

IN ENGLISH LITERATURE.

"As a mere literary monument, the English of the Bible remains the noblest example of the English tongue, while its perpetual use made it from the instant of its appearance the standard of our language."—*John Richard Green.*

CHAPTER X.

THE BIBLE IN ENGLISH LITERATURE.

THE hundred years which lie between 1550 and 1650 gave birth to more men who were destined to great literary distinction than has any other period of equal length in English history. To understand how true this is, it is only necessary that we try, for a moment, to conceive what our literature would be were that century dropped out of our annals. So much was it the flower and crown of the years which preceded it, and so much has it molded and inspired the years which have followed, that in case this century was lost, it is really hard to see what would be left. Never was nobler thought wedded to a richer tongue. This, indeed, was its special glory, and to this hour does it remain its supreme distinction. Recall the names of only a few of the writers who made this age illustrious. When was literary form finer, when was intellectual vigor more abundant? To lose that hundred years would be to lose Raleigh, who turned to literature after the most brilliant course ever run by a soldier of fortune, and doing so added fresh lustre to his renown; and Spenser, who gave his name to the stanza which errs only, if it err at all, by excess of sweetness; and Hooker, almost alone in the host of theologians for his command of stately prose; and Shakespeare, with the peerlessness of his range; and Isaac Walton, who represents the best speech of our daily life, and who has taught us how to bait our hook, in language which almost makes us envy the worm dying to such pleasant music; and Jeremy Taylor, the poet of the pulpit, and his rival, Robert South, who wielded as no other Englishman has the dangerous weapons of irony and scorn. Nor would the loss be any less in the sphere of thought. What should we do without Bacon, who makes science as clear as a summer brook; and quaint George Herbert, the most devout of our English poets; and Milton, who moved as masterfully among his words as Satan amid his legions; and Leighton, the divine, so rich in unction; and Owen, the theologian, more voluminous than luminous indeed, but treading serenely lofty levels of holy speculation; and Baxter, whose fervor glows forever in his impetuous appeals; and Bunyan, who, by virtue of his marvelous familiarity with the soul's pilgrimage, traveled all the road from Destruction to Deliverance, and closed with notes that even an angel before the throne might emulate? The loss of such a period as this hundred years would be not so much the loss of the keystone to the arch, as the loss of the arch itself, and that the centre-arch in the bridge of English literature. Where we looked for the highest point and the surest footing we should find, to our dismay, not a delightful thoroughfare, but only a dangerous chasm with a threatening torrent in its depths.

Now it was when this great century was at its full tide of literary splendor that the Authorized Version of the English Bible saw the light. At once it put itself into a place where it challenged comparison with the masterpieces of our tongue. How triumphantly it has stood the test, all the years since have shown. A sagacious critic of our own times expresses the universal conviction, when, speaking of it in the same breath with "The Divine Comedy" of Dante, Milton's "Paradise Lost," and Victor Hugo's "Les Miserables," he characterizes our English Bible as "great art." Addressing himself to those who might possibly make journalism their profession, Mr. Charles A. Dana, a master of his craft, has said lately: "There are some books that are absolutely indispensable to the kind of education that we are contemplating and to the profession that we are considering; and of all these the most indispensable, the most useful, the one whose knowledge is most effective, is the Bible. There is no book from which more valuable lessons can be learned. I am considering it now, not as a religious book, but as a manual of utility, of professional preparation and professional use for a journalist. There is, perhaps, no book whose style is more suggestive and more instructive, from which you learn more directly that sublime simplicity which never exaggerates, which recounts the greatest event with solemnity of course, but without sentimentality or affectation— none which you open with such confidence and lay down with such reverence : there is no book like the Bible."[1] Such estimates as these are only samples from the accumulating testimonies of men of high attainments to the worth of our English Bible as literature.

But we must not be understood as claiming for the language of the Bible in our hands to-day that it originated in the reign of James I. To do justice to the influence of this one book upon our literature, we must go much farther back than this. As the first sounds which the infant catches are often the syllables of some pious nursery rhyme, so our language listened in its earliest days to the very truths, and in many instances, to the very words now embalmed in our own Bible.

1. First of all, in our study of the influence of this book upon our literature, we must notice how powerfully it told upon the history of the language. Familiar as we are with the fact that in the present century Christian missionaries have in many instances made a language and a literature for

---

[1] Address at Union College, Schenectady, 1893.

the heathen nations to which they carried the gospel, it may not have occurred to us that very much the same process went on in Europe itself in the earlier years of our era. Ulfilas was not merely the apostle of Christianity to the Gothic race. Through his translation of the Scriptures into Gothic, he was also the father of Teutonic literature. This version—a portion of which is to-day the richest treasure in the library of the Swedish University of Upsala—is the greatest monument which Ulfilas himself reared to commemorate his success "as a way-breaker and a scholar. By it he became the first to raise a barbarian tongue to the dignity of a literary language; and the skill, knowledge, and adaptive ability it displays makes it the crowning testimony of his powers, as well as of his devotion to his work."[1] The work of Ulfilas was by no means singular. From the first the English Bible has been a conserving power in the English language. Carried down from one generation to another, the very vocabulary has been maintained to no little extent because it endeared itself to the aspirations, the passions, the confessions, the joys, and the griefs of the human soul. It is said that five-eighths of the language spoken by Alfred the Great circulates in England to-day, and who can question that it is largely to this one cause that this remarkable preservation

---

[1] "Encyc. Brit.," art. "Ulfilas."

must be ascribed? The very tongue that we speak is biblical; and by this we do not mean that it is the tongue of the Elizabethan or Jacobean times only or chiefly. "Its genealogy is to be traced up in a direct line through every state of biblical revision to the Latin Vulgate, and the common English ancestor of every such revision is the Wycliffite Bible of the fourteenth century."[1] Changing only its spelling, the Bible of John Wycliffe can be read by an Englishman now almost as readily as can the Bible of King James. In its turn, the Bible of Wycliffe was an evolution from versions earlier yet. Archbishop Cranmer claimed that many years before the Norman Conquest the book was "translated and read in the Saxon's tongue," and, although his statement was probably too sweeping, English literature still looks back across twelve centuries to the Venerable Bede consecrating his last hours to the translation of the Scriptures; and seeing the whole scholarship of the time summed up in him, honors Bede, in the well-known words of Edmund Burke, as "the father of English learning."

A. D. 1066. The Norman Conquest for a time checked the advance of letters. Even among the monks, scholars were few. For a hundred and fifty years after the battle of Hastings a little learning seems to have gone a long way.

---

[1] "Encyc. Brit.," art. "English Bible."

But another battle, not so speedily decided, was waging all this time between the vernaculars. Numbers of old words became obsolete. The versions of the Scriptures were invaluable in maintaining at this transition period the famous maxim of Horace, to be neither the last to use an old word, nor the first to use a new. Speaking of the Bible at this time, Cranmer says: "And when this language waxed old and out of common usage, because folk should not lack the fruit of reading, it was again translated into the newer language, whereof yet also many copies remain, and be daily found."[1] The revolution in the English tongue was not by any means a misfortune. The texture of the robe indeed remained the same, but it was now embroidered in gold and crimson, and resplendent with gems. Heard once more in the court, it was a richer language for the sea-change which it had suffered. Two centuries after the Conquest, the first Royal Proclamation in English was issued. In 1363, Parliament was opened by an English speech from the throne. Following the policy of quiet absorption, which the English nation has constantly pursued,—and that by no means in literature only,—the English tongue had taken into itself the best and richest elements of the Norman French; but the people in their common speech and popular ballads, had

A. D. 1248.

---

[1] "Encyc. Brit.," art. "English Bible."

never surrendered their vocabulary to the Conqueror.[1] The poetry of Chaucer is only one among many witnesses to the fact that all this while the words of the Bible were familiar in the ears of all sorts and conditions of Englishmen. Thus the language was molded to Wycliffe's hand when before the fourteenth century ran out he crowned its annals with his translation of the Scriptures. It will remain forever worthy of the consideration of the student of English literature that the two great versions of the Bible into the mother tongue appeared at the two great periods in the history of that tongue; in the reign of Richard II., when the language had recovered from the effects of the Norman Conquest, and grown rich by its experience, and in the reign of James I., when the glow and splendor of the Elizabethan era flung a robe before the advancing steps of Scripture more rare and splendid than that which Raleigh in the story laid at the feet of the "Virgin Queen."

The influence of Wycliffe's Bible on our English literature can scarcely be exaggerated. Lechler says that it marks an epoch in the development of the English language almost as much as Luther's translation does in the history of the German tongues.[2] To the historian Green, Wycliffe is as truly the father of our later English prose as

---
[1] Ward's "Chaucer," p. 19.
[2] Lechler's "Wycliffe," Vol. I., p. 347.

Chaucer of our later English poetry.[1] While the court poets were decorating their lines with the flowers of an exotic and artificial phraseology,[2] Wycliffe, and those associated with him, were preserving the strongest elements of the mother tongue; and so completely was this done that the great reformer probably deserves to be credited with the creation of a style, full of rough vigor, picturesque beauty, and crystalline clearness—a style to this hour "understanded of the people." Nor must we forget that Wycliffe—and even more than he, Tyndale—battled not only with the unwholesome fashions of the court, but also with the unscholarly prejudices of the clergy. We smile as we listen to the assumption of the Romish priest of to-day that "the old, unchangeable Church of Christ can have no more suitable alliance than that of her inseparable handmaid, the old, unchangeable, and well-deserving Latin."[3] But such words as these may serve to recall the struggle which, more than any other one book, Tyndale's new Bible ended between the ignorant masses of the clergy, who denounced Greek and Hebrew as the fatal sources of heathenism and Judaism,[4] and the new learning which insisted upon

---

[1] Green's "History," Vol. I., p. 489.
[2] Marsh, "Lectures on the English Language," p. 168.
[3] "The Stranger's Guide at High Mass," p. 4.
[4] Westcott, p. 164.

its right to draw the water of life straight from the fountain head. It is even more to our present purpose to remember that, as Professor George P. Marsh has said, Tyndale's translation of the New Testament has exerted "a more marked influence upon English philology than any other native work between the ages of Chaucer and Shakespeare." When, in due time, the Authorized Version came to be made, the translators seem to have exercised the greatest care in their choice of words. While many which they placed in the margin have become obsolete or provincial, very few such are to be found in the text itself. No doubt our English Bible has retained words in common use which might otherwise have been dropped; but to the taste of the translators is to be ascribed the fact that the language of the version made in the first years of the seventeenth century is so largely the language of our homes in the closing years of the nineteenth. Nor is the popular suspicion of change, which has been so abundantly shown in the case of the Revised Version, without a parallel in the history of the version which it revised. So sound a judge as John Selden complained of its un-English phrases. "Well enough," says he, "as long as scholars have to do with it; but when it comes among the common people, Lord, what gear do they make of it."[1] It would seem as much from

---

[1] Edgar, pp. 293, 328.

the earlier, as from later experiences through which versions of the Bible have passed, that the people themselves may be safely trusted to maintain the integrity of their richest national heirloom.

2. From the influence of the English Bible upon the history of the language, it is natural for us to pass to the influence which the book has exerted upon its character. What we are accustomed to term the biblical style, finds its fullest expression in the Authorized Version. But what is that version? The group of scholars who compiled it drew their vocabulary as they drew their translation, from all sources. If they had near at hand, while they worked the Great Bible and the Bishops' Bible, with which they would have the largest ecclesiastical sympathies, not less but rather more did they turn to the Bible of the Protestant exiles in Geneva, and of the Romanist recusants at Rheims. The Vulgate, on which Wycliffe had relied so largely, was in their counsels; and in using as they did the Bible of Thomas Matthew, they really pressed into the service the great names of Tyndale and Coverdale. Indeed, Tyndale's Version, it has been truly said, "is the parent of the authorized, as he himself is the true hero of the English Reformation."[1] Bishop Westcott has computed that nine-tenths of the Author-

---
[1] Angus, pp. 45, 46.

ized Version of 1 John, and five-sixths of the Ephesians are retained from Tyndale. The poor refugee, denied alike a home and a grave in his native land, influences our literature to-day more powerfully than any other one man, and is likely to continue to do so until the Bible of our childhood ceases to be read. To quote Mr. Froude: "The peculiar genius which breathes through it, the mingled tenderness and majesty, the Saxon simplicity, the preternatural grandeur, unequalled, unapproached in the attempted improvements of modern scholars—all are here, and bear the impress of one man, and that man William Tyndale."[1]

So free and natural is the translation in the Authorized Version, that we almost forget that it is a translation; and in truth, "it is not simply a translation, but a living reproduction of the original Scriptures in idiomatic English. It reads like an original work, such as the prophets and apostles might have written in the seventeenth century for English readers. It reveals an easy mastery of the rich resources of the English language, and blends with singular felicity, Saxon force and Latin melody."[2] This is itself evidence of the highest art. So thoroughly is the rendering naturalized among us, that we have

---
[1] Froude's "History of England," Vol. III, p. 84.
[2] Roberts "Companion," etc., p. 89.

come to think that the effort of the translators could not have been so great after all. The very words of the original must have lent themselves at once to translation. It is well for us to remember the protest of Cardinal Newman: "Scripture easy of translation? Then, why have there been so few good translators? Why is it that there has been such great difficulty in combining the two necessary qualities—fidelity to the original and purity in the adopted vernacular? Why is it that the authorized versions of the church are often so inferior to the original as compositions, except that the church is bound, above all things, to see that the version is doctrinally correct, and in a difficult problem, is obliged to put up with defects in what is of secondary importance, provided she secure what is of first? And, then, Scripture not elaborate! Scripture not ornamented in diction and musical in cadence! Why, consider the Epistle to the Hebrews! Where is there in the classics any composition more carefully, more artistically written? Consider the book of Job; is it not a sacred drama, as artistic, as perfect, as any great tragedy of Sophocles or Euripides? Consider the Psalter; are there no ornaments, no rhythm, no studied cadences, no responsive members in that divinely beautiful book "[1]

Why should we hesitate to say that in the

---

[1] Newman, John Henry, "Idea of a University," pp. 288, 289.

choice of language for his translation, Tyndale had help from on high? He had given up his life to his work; for the love he bore this word of God, he had consented to be exiled, persecuted, imprisoned; he was a man of prayer, and spent his hours in close communion with his Lord. The vocabulary of such a man seems almost sacred. What is certain is, that Tyndale's words are largely the words of our version to-day, and his spirit breathes through the whole. "He felt," says Bishop Westcott, "by a happy instinct, the potential affinity between Hebrew and English idioms, and enriched our language and thought forever with the characteristics of the Semitic mind."[1] If to the mingled blood in the veins of the English people we attribute in such a large measure the national greatness, equally does the English Bible owe to the various hands that labored on its vocabulary the happy blending of contrasted elements which makes it such a noble model of style. We are told that it is worth while to master Spanish, so as to be able to read Cervantes, and Italian for the sake of Dante. How much are we to be envied, who are accustomed from our cradles to the tongue into which our Bible is rendered! We need not go the length of the poet Swinburne, who considers that the New Testament gained, beyond all power of

---
[1] Wescott, p. 211

expression, in being translated out of the original Greek "into divine English," in order to appreciate the advantage to the people at large of this matchless version. But we are bound to do full justice to the fact that there can be no writer of any eminence who has entirely escaped its influence. Those unconscious years in which we gather our vocabulary, and store up the words which through all after life stay with us, have been in England and America for more than ten centuries and a half, familiar with this great masterpiece of English prose. A comparison of our literature from John Bunyan to John Ruskin with the literature of France in a like period, would be sufficient to show that we owe more than we can ever tell to our early training in the English of the Bible. The character of our national tongue has been tempered by it; and to it our great writers are largely indebted for the sobriety, the strength, and the sweetness which distinguish their best efforts.

3. This leads us to consider more in detail, the influence of the English Bible on the literature of our language. The subject is very extensive, but we must find space for some illustrations of this influence, both direct and indirect. The student of Shakespeare will be impressed with the extent to which his dramas are permeated with the very phraseology of Scripture. Evidently

before the Authorized Version was made, the Bible was a household word in England. The hospitable memory of the poet must have borne away from his early home in Stratford-on-Avon, great portions of Scripture. Bishop Wordsworth considers that we may "put together our best authors who have written upon subjects not professedly religious or theological, and we shall not find in them all united so much evidence of the Bible having been read and used as we have found in Shakespeare alone."[1] Often he quotes closely the words of the Bible, as where Humphrey, Duke of Gloster, cries:

> Mine eyes are full of tears, my heart of grief.
> Ah! Humphrey, this dishonor in thine age,
> Will bring thy head with sorrow to the ground;

or when Benedick is praised in that

> From the crown of his head to the sole of his foot,

he is all mirth. With the characters of the Bible he is familiar. Satan and Pharaoh and Samson and Solomon and David and Herod and Pilate and Paul are not names only in his ears, but he understands their natures and their doings as well as he understands the kings, the warriors, the heroes, and the heroines whom he marshalls on his stage. His commendation of his

---

[1] "Shakespeare and the Bible," p. 345. To this book I am indebted for many of the references on this subject.

soul to his Saviour in his last will is, we dare believe, more than a mere legal form, and shows him as in spirit a follower of

> . . . Those blessed feet,
> Which fourteen hundred years ago, were nailed
> For our advantage on the bitter cross.

No doubt Shakespeare had to the full the faculty of merging his own distinctive individuality in that of his characters. Of him personally we know little. But the strong religious sentiments which he puts into the mouths of others must have come in the great majority of instances from his own heart, and must express his own convictions. As such, these sentiments possess a peculiar interest. They throw a valuable light upon that many-minded nature which was content to be seen by all time in any guise rather than its own. And they are of even greater importance if we think of them as the sentiments of multitudes of Englishmen at that time. The work of Wycliffe and his simple preachers, of Tyndale and Coverdale and Cranmer, had not been lost. The country was now in the hold of the Bible. We turn then to the dramas of Shakespeare as the most powerful expression of popular English religious thought —the thought of the yeoman, the merchant, the artisan.

The Genevan theologian could not have put more strongly the doctrine of the Divine sovreignty and a particular providence. We recall at once the famous lines in "Hamlet":

> There's a Divinity that shapes our ends,
> Rough-hew them how we will.

But not less clear is Queen Katharine's faith:

> Heaven is above all yet: there sits a Judge
> That no king can corrupt.

The words of Scripture, and equally the comforting truth which they express, are heard in "Hamlet" again:

> There is a special providence in the fall of a sparrow.

Surely the poet himself speaks in that impressive utterance of pious Henry VI.:

> O Thou, that judgest all things, stay my thoughts
> If my suspect be false, forgive me, God:
> For judgment only doth belong to Thee.

The speech of Portia is an English classic, but it puts as truly as any preacher could that love which redeemed the world:

> Mercy is above this scepter'd sway;
> It is enthroned in the heart of kings;
> It is an attribute of God himself;
> And earthly power doth then show likest God's
> When mercy seasons justice.

The very words of Paul to the Ephesians (Eph. 1 : 7) must have been in the poet's mind when he makes Clarence in the Tower speak of:

> Redemption
> Through Christ's dear blood, shed for our grievous sin.

And the lines in the "Two Gentlemen of Verona,"

> Who by repentance is not satisfied
> Is not of heaven nor earth; for these are pleased,

sound like the refrain of the parable of the Prodigal Son.

When Tennyson sings:

> And ah! for a man to rise in me
> That the man I am may cease to be,

he has been anticipated by Shakespeare:

> Strange it is
> That nature must compel us to lament
> Our most persisted deeds;

and both of them no doubt recalled Paul's passionate cry: "O wretched man that I am! who shall deliver me from the body of this death!" (Rom. 7 : 24).

It is not hard to believe that the sublime lament of Job, "I go whence I shall not return, even to the land of darkness and the shadow of death" (Job 10 : 21), inspired the masterly suggestion of

> The undiscovered country from whose bourn
> No traveler returns;

and that his remembrance of Ecclesiastes (ch. 12 : 7) dictated to the dramatist the last words of King Richard II. :

> Mount, mount my soul! thy seat is up on high;
> While my gross flesh sinks downward here to die.

The devout life must have had a true meaning to the man who could write:

> In peace there's nothing so becomes a man
> As modest stillness and humility;

and it must have drawn its impulse from the very teachings of Him who was meek and lowly in spirit, teachings which are heard with no uncertain sound in many of the lines which make the poet's utterances familiar in our mouths as household words. Time forbids our enlarging upon Shakespeare's use of Scripture; but perhaps enough has been said to show to what an extent the language and the thought of the greatest masterpieces of literature in our tongue are indebted to the English Bible.

From the dramatist we may turn to the romancist. The British novel cannot be studied apart from the influence which the Bible has had upon it. The name of Walter Scott will occur at once. His intimacy with the very words of Scripture dated from his childhood, and found an illustration when, only a boy at the high school of Edinburgh, he ventured to assert that the word *with* is in one place used as a noun and not as a preposition, quoting correctly the verse from Judges, "And Samson said unto Delilah, If they bind me with seven green withs that were never dried, then shall I be weak, and be as another man" (Judg. 16 : 7). And it continued until the very end, when he called for the Bible to be read to him as the one book for that solemn hour, and found comfort where so many others have found and will find it in the fourteenth chapter of the Gospel of John.

To Scott there was perpetual music in the national Psalm book; his ear delighted in the magnificent imagery of the prophets; he was familiar not only with the heroes of the Bible, but with its less-known characters; his stories—"Waverly," "Old Mortality," "The Bride of Lammermoor," "Ivanhoe," illustrated great religious truths; every reference to the sacred pages was caught up and cherished by a Bible-loving people; and, while his range of choice passed through all the books from Genesis to Revelation, he used most and to the highest purpose the words and scenes of the Evangelists.[1] Hundreds, and probably thousands of verses from the Bible could be rescued from his romances, and the indirect allusions which take for granted an acquaintance with the Scriptures on the part of his readers are more numerous far. The same appreciation of the Bible has marked later writers of fiction. When Walter Savage Landor, praising Charles Dickens' style, asks him where he got it, the novelist replied instantly: "Why, from the New Testament, to be sure."

---

[1] See "The Bible in Waverly," by Nicholas Dickson, Edinburgh, 1884.

An over-sensitive reader of his last and unfinished story ventured to remonstrate with him on what seemed to be a lack of reverence in a Scripture quotation. Dickens answered: "I have always striven in my writing to express veneration for the life and lessons of our Saviour, because I feel it; and I rewrote that history for my children—every one of whom knew it from hearing it repeated to them long before they could read, and almost as soon as they could speak." His readers will remember with what wonderful skill he wrought the words of Scripture into his own somewhat artificial rhetoric, as though he felt sufficiently mistrustful of himself to welcome the aid of the established standard of English style. But in the crowning scene of "The Tale of Two Cities"—the work in which he touched his very highest point— it was a still nobler impulse, one thinks, which prompted his choice of a text. The castaway, Sydney Carton, by his voluntary death, better than any other character in English fiction, illustrates the Master's word, "Greater love hath no man than this, that a man lay down his life for his friends" (John 15 : 13). He is upon the scaffold, in the wild days of the French Revolution. A poor little seamstress, innocent as he, and to him, until that tragic meeting, a stranger, is to die also; but in that hour she remembers a cousin of hers in the sweet far-away country, ignorant of the dreadful doom by which she is now to perish, and in her simplicity she turns to Sydney, for light on the one question which perplexes her. "'Do you think,'" and the uncomplaining eyes in which there is so much endurance fill with tears, and the lips part a little more and tremble, "'that it will seem long to me while I wait for her in the better land where I trust both you and I will be mercifully sheltered.'

"'It cannot be, my child; there is no Time there, and no trouble there.'

"'You comfort me so much! I am so ignorant. Am I to kiss you now? Is the moment come?'

"'Yes.'

"She kisses his lips; he kisses hers; they solemnly bless each other. The spare hand does not tremble as he releases it; nothing worse than a sweet, bright constancy is in the patient face. She goes next before him—is gone.

"'I am the Resurrection and the Life, saith the Lord; he that believeth in me, though he were dead, yet shall he live; and whosoever liveth and believeth in me, shall never die.'

"'The murmuring of many voices, the upturning of many faces, the pressing on of many footsteps in the outskirts of the crowd, so that it swells forward in a mass, like one great heave of water, all flashes away."

With his more natural style, Thackeray made even a better use of the English Bible than did Dickens. His best known romance owed its title to Bunyan, and found its points of view in Ecclesiastes. There is no more pathetic chapter in "Vanity Fair" than that in which the widowed mother, driven by poverty, prepares to give up her boy to his ungenial grandfather; and it is inspired from a chapter not less pathetic in the childhood of Samuel: "That night Amelia made the boy read the story of Samuel to her, and how Hannah, his mother, having weaned him, brought him to Eli the high priest, to minister before the Lord. And he read the song of gratitude which Hannah sang, and which says, 'Who it is who maketh poor and maketh rich, and bringeth low and exalteth—how the poor shall be raised up out of the dust, and how, in his own might, no man shall be strong.' Then he read how Samuel's mother made him a little coat, and brought it to him from year to year when she came up to offer the yearly sacrifice. And then, in her sweet, simple way, George's mother made commentaries to the boy upon this affecting story. How Hannah, though she loved her son so much, yet gave him up because of her vow. And how she must always have thought of him as she sat at home, far away, making the little coat; and Samuel, she was sure, never forgot his mother; and how happy she must have been as the time came—and the years pass away very quickly—when she should see her boy, and how good and wise he had grown. This little sermon she spoke with a gentle, solemn voice, and dry eyes, until she came to the account of their meeting—then the discourse broke off suddenly, the tender heart overflowed, and taking the boy to her breast, she rocked him in her arms, and wept silently over him in a sainted agony of tears." [1]

When the great novelist comes to draw the noblest of all his characters, Colonel Newcome—and who has probably no superior in all the portrait gallery of English fiction—the spirit of Him who was "the first true gentleman that ever lived" is constantly apparent. Our step is quiet and our voice falls to a whisper, as we stand at his bedside, when for him the last moment has come. "At the usual evening hour the chapel bell began to toll, and Thomas Newcome's hands outside the bed feebly beat time. And just as the last bell struck, a peculiar sweet smile shone over his face, and he lifted up his head a little and quickly said 'Adsum,' and fell back. It was the word we used at school when names were called; and lo, he whose heart was as that of a little child, had answered to his name, and stood in the presence of the Master." [2]

---

[1] "Vanity Fair."   [2] "The Newcomes."

Over the whole course of English poetry since the Elizabethan period, the Bible has exerted a marked and wholesome influence. If there are decidedly unscriptural elements in Milton's "Ode to the Nativity," if the theology of "Paradise Lost" is any different from the theology of the book from which it professed to get its inspiration, if imagination more than authority, dictated "Samson Agonistes," it cannot be denied that the mind of their author was most powerfully influenced by the Bible, and certainly the Psalms suggested the one fine hymn (written when he was fifteen years of age) which Milton has bequeathed to our collections :

> Let us with a gladsome mind
> Praise the Lord, for he is kind.

Joseph Addison is remembered to-day, not so much because he was the writer of limpid and graceful prose as because he was the singer of another of the few hymns for which our congregations have to thank the English poets; and that hymn is itself a paraphrase of the nineteenth Psalm.[1]

But it is when we leave the age of rhetorical artifice, and breathe the purer air of natural sentiment, that we understand how great the power of our Bible has been in the history of our poetry. Mr. Stopford A. Brooke does not exaggerate when

---

[1] "The Spacious Firmament on High," etc.

he claims Cowper as the poet who roused passion from its long slumber, and struck the first note of that personal poetry which was afterward carried so far in the "Prelude" of Wordsworth, the "Alastor" of Shelley, the "Childe Harold" of Byron; and he is no doubt correct when he says, "It was the great religious movement led by the Wesleys, joined afterward by the fiery force of Whitefield, which descended through Newton to the hymns and poetry of Cowper."[1] That movement, we need scarcely add, was intensely biblical. It caught and carried on the inspiration of the day of Pentecost. It took its marching orders from the Great Commission itself. Cowper's best hymns are those which are the most biblical, as it was to the Bible that he owed the few clear skies which arched his clouded and melancholy course. Upon him, as well as upon most of our great poets since he struck the key-note of a simple and more natural style, the direct influence of the Bible is very apparent. The very words of Scripture are woven into their lines. It was Jeremiah who gave Byron the hint for his grand and gloomy sketch "Darkness"; it was Job that suggested "Thanatopsis" to Bryant. But for Paul's great chapter on the resurrection of the dead, we should never have had Wordsworth's "Ode to Immortality." Tennyson was evidently a diligent student of the

---
[1] "Theology of the English Poets," pp. 11, 12.

Bible. He assured Dr. Samuel Cox that he held Job to be the greatest poem whether of ancient or modern times;[1] and with its most musical words he concludes the most popular of his earlier compositions, when the sick girl tells her mother that she hopes before long:

> To lie within the light of God, as I lie upon your breast—
> And the wicked cease from troubling, and the weary are at rest.

What is still more interesting and equally to our purpose is the use which he more than once made of Peter's inspiring words: "Whom having not seen, ye love; in whom, though now ye see him not, yet believing, ye rejoice with joy unspeakable and full of glory" (1 Peter 1 : 8). It is with these words in his mind that Tennyson opens the poem which, more than any other, expresses the deeper feeling of his century:

> Strong Son of God, immortal Love,
>   Whom we, that have not seen thy face,
>   By faith, and faith alone embrace,
> Believing, where we cannot prove!

and when the poem closes, some echo from the same mighty assurance seems to linger with him yet, as he reverts to "That friend of mine who lives in God":

> That God, which ever lives and loves;
>   One God, one law, one element,
>   And one far-off divine event,
> To which the whole creation moves.

---

[1] "Freeman," April 7, 1893.

But we have done scant justice to the Bible in English literature when we have traced its direct influence alone. Quotations from our great writers couched in the precise words of Scripture it would be an easy matter to multiply; and yet there would lie before us the unreaped field of richer promise from which we should need harvest in the scriptural allusions and references which, if less direct, are not less obvious. The Bible not only pushes itself up like the rock penetrating the surface, but like the rock again it tinges and fertilizes the soil which lies all about it. The childhood of our great writers, in the majority of instances, has been lived in an atmosphere familiar with the rhetoric of Scripture. As Dr. A. P. Peabody once said: "Our Bible is still the key to the best English diction; and by conversance with it our children are made familiar with their own language in a purer form than any other which can be placed before them."[1] Who shall say how the public reading of this book has trained the people of England and America to a knowledge of melody, and to a love for harmonious prose? To this daily discipline, coupled with the enforced learning of the fine old Scotch paraphrases, Mr. Ruskin says he owes the first cultivation of his ear in sound. The translators of our Authorized Version lived too near the melodious age in our literature

---

[1] "The Deathless Book," David O'Mears, D. D., p. 195.

to dare offend this fine sense of harmony, and in many cases they introduced changes only for the sake of pleasant cadence in reading.[1] More than this: To be conversant with the Bible is to be trained not alone to shrink from discordant arrangement of words, but also in the whole art of suitable expression. To this hour our Bible remains the best handbook of rhetoric. So Robert South could write with characteristic force and beauty: "Where do we find such rhetoric and poetry as in the Scripture, or such pathos as in the Lamentations of Jeremy? One would think that every word was the noise of a breaking heart. So that he who said he would not read the Scriptures for fear of spoiling his style, showed himself as much a blockhead as an atheist." Its influence upon a style originally deficient in the essentials of distinction has been illustrated within a few years in the experience of Mr. Stanley, the African explorer. Of him a competent writer asks: "Where did he get his present style?" and then procceded to answer his own question, thus: "A clue may be found in his own story of the Bible which Sir William Mackinnon gave him at starting. He read it through, he tells us, three times. . . . He has read, I will venture to guess, the greater prophets of the Old Testament and the epistles in the New Testament, till his mind has

---

[1] Edgar, p. 305.

become saturated with them. There is no imitation of any of these writers, or no conscious imitation . . . But they have modified his habits of thought and his methods of expression. He has brooded over them in the recesses of his awful forest till they have become part of his spiritual and part of his intellectual life."[1]

For furnishing the writer or the speaker with words suited to his purpose, there is no other book in the English language worthy to be named in the same breath with the Bible. As Milton says: "There are no songs comparable to the songs of Zion, no orations equal to those of the prophets, and no politics like those the Scriptures teach." How much this is the case the history of oratory abundantly proves. Edmund Burke's habit was to read a chapter in Isaiah before going to speak in the House of Commons. "Isaiah," he says, "possessed both the blaze of eloquence and the light of truth." Daniel Webster was a constant student of the Bible, and his most impressive use of the 139th Psalm in one of his great cases will be quoted so long as his name is remembered. "A sense of duty pursues us ever. It is omnipresent like the Deity. If we take to ourselves the wings of the morning and dwell in the uttermost parts of the sea, duty performed or duty violated, is still with us for our happiness or our misery. If we

---

[1] "New York Tribune," May 28, 1890.

say, *surely the darkness shall cover us*, in the darkness as in the light our obligations are yet with us. We cannot escape their power, nor fly from their presence." A few moments before he died, his mind went back to the brightest hour in all the history of our world, and he was heard to say: "*Peace on earth and good will to men*—that is the happiness, the essence—*good will toward men.*"

The noblest English orator of our century, John Bright, knew his Bible well. He heard it as a child at home; he took his first lessons from a Baptist minister, made some of his earliest addresses in the Baptist chapel of his native town, and more than once acknowledged that it was to a Baptist preacher he was indebted for the most useful hints he ever received on the art of public speaking. In his own family there was no book which he loved to read aloud more than the Bible,[1] and in his speeches there are abundant evidences of his familiarity with its language. On one memorable occasion he added a new figure to the phrase book of the House of Commons, when he said of an opponent: "The right hon. gentleman has retired into what may be called his political cave of Adullam, and he has called about him

---

[1] Mr. Bright's favorite passages from the Bible included the Beatitudes; Eph. 6: 10–20; 1 Cor. 13; Exod. 20: 1–17; Eccl. 11: 1–10; and Ps. 27.

every one that was in distress, and every one that was discontented." "An Adullamite," from that hour to this, has been a political malcontent; and a few days after, Mr. Lowe, one of those included in Mr. Bright's invective, had to make the humiliating confession, that he had been besieged with inquiries from members of the House anxious to hear where and what this "cave of Adullam" was. While enlightening their ignorance of Scripture at his own expense, he said he was reminded of the dying eagle when he discovered that the arrow with which his heart had been pierced was furnished with feathers taken from his own wing.

It was probably for the sake of its clearness of language that the "book of Proverbs" attracted the special notice of Edward Everett, who made a constant study of it for rhetorical purposes. For nervous force quite as much as for clearness, the vocabulary of the Bible is remarkable. Listen to Sir Walter Raleigh: "I have considered, saith Solomon, all the works that are under the sun, and behold all is vanity and vexation of spirit; but who believes it till Death tells it us? Oh eloquent, just, and mighty Death; whom none could advise, thou hast persuaded; what none hath dared, thou hast done; and whom all the world hath flattered, thou only hast cast-out of the world and despised; thou hast drawn together all the far-stretched greatness, all the pride, cruelty, and ambition of men; and covered it all over with these two narrow words, *Hic Jacet.*"

In our own century no two authors are more marked by literary strength than Carlyle and Ruskin. What Carlyle wrote to Ruskin about one of his books, "It is all written with the old nobleness and fire in which no other living voice to my knowledge equals yours," Ruskin might with equal truth have written to Carlyle. Both of them are biblical in their choice of words. Once while visiting at a country house, Carlyle was requested to conduct family worship, and it is said, that having begun reading the book of Job he read it right through to the end. "One of the grandest things," he says of it, "ever written with a pen." Toward the close of his life he sat waiting for tea one evening, with a Bible in his hand, and was heard repeating to himself the hymn dear no doubt from its early associations :

> The hour of my departure comes,
> I hear the voice that calls me home;
> At last O Lord, let trouble cease,
> And let thy servant die in peace.

Then, all unconscious that he was observed, he buried himself once more in the pages of that same book of Job, of which he had once said : "Sublime sorrow, sublime reconciliation ; oldest choral melody as of the heart of mankind—so soft and great, as the summer midnight, as the world with its seas and stars." And about how much besides the book of Job is it true that the soft and the great mingle in the vocabulary of Scripture. Benjamin Franklin read Habakkuk to a literary circle in Paris, winning the unanimous tribute of admiration for an author of whom not one of them had ever heard before ; and Samuel Johnson, in a London club, introduced his friends to a pastoral which he said he had lately met with, and which they imagined had only just been composed ; and when they were all loud in their praises of its simple and pathetic beauty he informed them that it was only the story of Ruth which he had read them from a book called the Bible, that they all affected to despise. John Bright's happy use of another Scripture idyl has now taken its place among the immortal passages in our English prose. It was when explaining why he, a simple Friend, had accepted office in the British Government that he said : "There is a passage in the Old Testament which has often struck me as being one of great beauty. Many of you will recollect that the prophet, in journeying to and fro, was very hospitably entertained by one termed in the Bible a Shunammite woman. In return for her hospitality he wished to make her some amends, and he called her to him and asked her what there was he should do for her. *Shall I speak for thee to the king*, he said, *or to the captain of the host?* Now it has always appeared to me that the Shunammite woman returned a great answer. She replied, in declining the prophet's offer, *I dwell among mine own people.* When the question was put to me whether I would step into the position in which I now find myself, the answer from my heart was the same—I wish to dwell among mine own people."

The clearness and vigor of our English Bible are not more remarkable than its beauty and delicacy. It has been repeatedly noticed about John Bunyan, that rude by birth and nurture, living a wild and profligate life for many years and writing in an age of unparalleled literary licentiousness, there is not a line in all his works which the most refined taste of to-day could wish to see blotted out. Doubtless the explanation may be found in the fact that it was in the Bible that Bunyan found his masculine melodious prose, and as Coleridge has truly said, intense study of that one book will keep any writer from being vulgar. In humble homes, under unkindly circumstances, among rough and ignoble and emphatically commonplace associations, the Bible is like the prison flower—persistent in its blossoming, or the hymns with which Paul and Silas challenged the shame of the inner dungeon and the suffering of the stocks. There was an instinctive sense of the fitness of things in the old lady in Edinburgh of whom Sir Walter Scott tells us, that although she had fallen into poor circumstances, and was forced to live in a room on the highest stairs of Covenant Close, she never read her chapter except out of a Cambridge Bible, printed in the best style of the art and bound in embroidered velvet.

4. Language, however, is first and foremost a vehicle for thought. The greatness of literary art no doubt depends, as Mr. Walter Pater affirms, "on the quality of the matter it informs or controls." Our subject would be very incomplete were we to say nothing about the influence of our English Bible upon the intellectual vigor and richness of the language. What Mr. Froude observes as to Tyndale, in his eloquent eulogy on him, is true of the book which to so large an extent still bears his impress: "His spirit, as it were divorced from the world, moved in a purer element than common air." Very noticeable is the absence of all affectation or self-consciousness in its style. The aim of the translators is simply to convey their message, and in no single instance do they turn aside to call attention to themselves. What may be called Bible periods in history have been periods of intellectual renaissance. Thought has never been fresher than then. The fall of Constantinople in 1453 sent culture westward, an exile welcome to the quickened intellectual life of Italy,

and it was then that with greater freedom of thought came a revived interest in the New Testament. "Greece arose from the dead with the New Testament in her hand."[1] Of the Greek Testament of Erasmus it has been said that "it contributed more to the liberation of the human mind from the thralldom of the clergy than all the uproar and rage of Luther's many pamphlets." Wycliffe was himself the foremost champion of free thought of his times in England. In other countries the human intellect was claiming liberty to read in the vernacular that law of the Lord which made wise the simple, and it was claiming it not in vain. "We will not," shouted one sturdy English speaker, "be the dregs of all, seeing other nations have the law of God, which is the law of our faith, written in their tongue." "Frenchmen, Belgians, and Normans," wrote Purvey in his prologue to the revised edition of Wycliffe's Bible, 1388, "have the Bible . . . translated in here modir language: Why shulden not Englishmen have the same in here modir language, I can not wite."[2] When the full tide of the Protestant Reformation reached England, it brought with it the revival of learning, and as we have already remarked, our Authorized Version shone out on the firmament of letters at the very period when the sky was all ablaze with the splendor of great stars.

---

[1] "Our Bible," Canon Talbot, p. 59.   [2] Edgar, p. 4.

No doubt there was both action and reaction. The period of intellectual quickening gave an impulse to the study of the Bible, while at the same time it received an impulse from it. But what especially concerns us, is to recognize that the Bible has never been driven into the background at such periods. It has taken its place in the van of every advance movement in the world of literature, from the fall of Constantinople until now. It has been the first to find and the earliest to welcome the light breeze which always springs up at the dawn.

Not less remarkable has been the wide and generous range of thought which the English Bible has affected. Lord Bacon stands at the head of an illustrious host of scientific men who have refused to divorce their favorite studies from the teachings of this book. Sir Isaac Newton interested himself in questions of prophecy ; Sir David Brewster claimed Scripture as his ally in his discussion with Whewell on the plurality of worlds, while his opponent had long before that time distinguished himself in the field of natural theology ; Faraday, the leading chemist of his day, expounded the Bible every Sunday in the meeting house of an obscure sect ; in the presence of the same volume, his master, Sir Humphry Davy, a member of almost all the scientific institutions in the world, became as docile as a little child ; and the genial Sedgwick, amid his fearless geological researches, kept pure and true the loyalty of his boyhood to the story of Genesis.

The achievements of art, even more than the fairy tales of science, have been inseparably associated with the Bible. The Scriptorium in the monastery was often a veritable studio. Manuscript copies of the Gospels remain to this day rich in gem and gold, and gorgeous in their blazonry of bright colors; and often the masterpiece of the pious transcriber was a very miracle of beauty. In our own time, no picture has more powerfully affected English art than Holman Hunt's lovely figure of "Christ the Light of the World." That picture, as the artist has lately told us, is the memorial of his own conversion. It was in the period of a spiritual struggle waged within a singularly sensitive nature, that this conception came to the young painter. "Youth," he says, "offered me bribes on both sides—pleasures of the material or of the spiritual kind—and as I was weighing all, I came upon the text, 'Behold, I stand at the door and knock.' . . The figure of Christ standing at the door haunted me, gradually coming in more clearly defined meaning, waiting in the night—ever night near the dawn; with a light sheltered from chance of extinction in a lantern; with a crown on his head, bearing that also of thorns; with body robed like a priest, but in a world with signs of neglect and blindness. You will say that it was an emotional conversion, but there were other influences outside of sentiment. . . Many times since that day, when the critics assailed it violently, I have been comforted by hearing of persons in sickness who knew not the painter's name, and troubled themselves not at all about the manner of its production or the artistic question, speaking of the picture as one that had haunted them and given them hope —the hope that makes death have no terrors. It is not egotism that makes me pleased at this. I look to it as one of the testimonies—a very little one—of the greatness and the necessity of the creed it illustrates. . . From the little beginning of Abraham's leaving Padan-aram, the whole of the active-minded people of the world have been blessed with an inspiring religion, which has endowed Shakespeare and the poor in the hospital equally with noble and patient hope."

In our literature, what book has been found comparable to the English Bible in stimulating thought? When Hugh Miller, the Scottish stonemason, destined to be the literary leader of the Disruption, comes to look back over his life, he remembers that what wakened his mind and made him conscious of thought, was the history of Joseph. And the truth in reference to one is also the truth in reference to multitudes. The Bible has stimulated thought in whole communities, and it is doing so yet. Washington Irving is not singular in his experience when he says: "I think I have waked a good many sleeping fancies by the reading of a chapter in Isaiah"; and Hawthorne speaks on behalf of many besides himself when he confesses that the Bible and the "Pilgrim's Progress" are the main sources of his inspiration. Indeed, could Job and David, Isaiah and Ezekiel, muster their literary children only, could the evangelists and Paul summon from our shelves the volumes which have sprung from their kindling words, we should find ourselves in the midst of a vast and radiant host. Spenser met his Red Cross Knight in the Ephesians. Milton's genius caught fire in the garden of Eden and on the Mountain of Temptation; while to the larger hope of the Christian creed, Tennyson is indebted for "In Memoriam." The melodies of Byron and Moore, and the labored descriptive poems of Willis, draw their text from Bible incidents. It is difficult to conceive of Cowper apart from the influence which the same book exerted over him. It stirred the tranquil nature of Wordsworth in his most heroic moments; the early training in Bible text and teaching went far to make a theologian of Robert Browning; while Emerson and Longfellow, Lowell and Whittier, are children either of the manse or of the meeting-house.

Nor is it in stimulating thought alone that our English Bible has had so great power. Equally has it molded and controlled the thought which it has first aroused. It was the constant companion of Abraham Lincoln when he worked a bare-footed boy in the field, and there are passages in his last inaugural which sound as though he penned them just after rising from its pages. When John Bright said that he was willing to stake the divine origin of the whole Bible upon the "Psalter," he had undoubtedly in his mind the wonderful influence which that book had exerted over his own impetuous and ardent nature. Henry M. Stanley says that the words, "Whatsoever thy hand findeth to do, do it with thy might," have become the guiding motto of his life. It is under the spell of Isaiah that Handel rises to unexpected grandeur, and his servant testifies that at the time when the great master was composing "The Messiah," he often saw his tears mingled with the ink. "I did think," Handel himself said in his broken English, "I did see all heaven before me, and the great God himself." When the Great Bible was printed its powerful influence was speedily recognized. It drove the impure literature from the field as bats and owls—creatures of the night—fly before the sun. From that time to this, national morality has been gauged by national appreciation of the Scriptures. We may reasonably believe that it was Paul's great words to the Philippians (Phil. 3 : 13), that taught Arthur Hugh Clough to sing :

> For still we hope
> That in a world of larger scope;
> What here is faithfully begun
> Will be completed, not undone;

as it was certainly the words of the Apostle John (1 John 2 : 1) that steadied the soul of Sir Walter Raleigh when, after wild and stormy experiences his days of pilgrimage drew to a close, and in the immediate prospect of the scaffold he could look beyond to the final court of decision :

> For there Christ is the King's attorney,
> Who pleads for all without degrees,
> And he hath angels, but no fees.
> And when the grand twelve-million jury
> Of our sins, with direful fury,
> 'Gainst our souls black verdicts give,
> Christ pleads his death, and then we live.[1]

Indeed, when we remember how vast the influence of this book has been ; how it has corrected error ; how it has controlled passion ; how it has molded thought ; how it has anticipated periods of intellectual awakening in the nation ; how it has bent over the cradle of genius ; how it has held with firm, yet gentle hands, the impetuous aspiration of fancy ; how it has enlarged the sphere of

---

[1] Sir Walter Raleigh. "My Pilgrimage." 1603.

science, until exact thought has touched the boundaries of speculation, and the philosopher has discovered himself to be a poet; when we remember all this, it can scarcely excite in us any surprise that men have been tempted to offer to the book a homage which belongs of right only to its Author. Few famous sentences have been more often quoted, and few indeed quoted to worse purpose, than Chillingworth's memorable exclamation: "The Bible I say, the Bible only, is the religion of Protestants."[1] The historian of civilization, Henry Thomas Buckle, does not hesitate to credit the book in which these words occur, with having shaped the thought of the century in which it was uttered. But the spirit of liberality for which Chillingworth was so conspicuous, and the broad and philosophic character of his mind, should be for all times a sufficient corrective to any narrow and unworthy interpretation of his memorable words. In the face of Chillingworth's history, a convert to Rome and then returning with full personal conviction to the purer faith, it is not difficult to understand his meaning. As much as Wycliffe or Tyndale, he appeals against human authority; and declares that the book in which God speaks to us directly, whether by the prophets of the Old Dispensation, or by his Son in the New, is to be the source of our light.

---

[1] Chillingworth's "Works," p. 481.

"Christ, and Christ alone; Christ the Son of God revealing the Father; Christ, by the Holy Spirit, made real to the believer; Christ, and Christ alone, is the religion of Protestantism."[1]

The excursions which we have been making into the realms of literature, science, and art must now cease; but only because our time bids us pause. The subject itself is almost boundless. Our survey should leave with us the persuasion that, while other things are soon forgotten, the Bible remains; while other things grow old, this book carries in its heart the secret of perpetual youth. Every year, it has been said, buries its own literature. The book that lasts a decade is rare indeed, the book which outlives its century is unique. The masterpieces of our language can be placed on a very few shelves. But the English Bible seems to be superior to the ebb and flow of popular fancy and of critical opinion. It has been remarked that even those who with George Eliot abandon their early faith go on reading the Scriptures for the sake of their intellectual charm. Few things are more pathetic in her journal than the half apology with which the author of "Romola" confesses to purchasing a large print Bible in her old age, and finding comfort from its pages.

There is an element of permanence even in the language of the Bible. Its vocabulary is colloquial

---

[1] R. H. Horton, D. D.

without being familiar, and dignified without being stilted. No version in any language seems to have found its way to the national heart so completely as that for which we are indebted to the reign of James I. Later attempts at revision have sometimes commended themselves to the judgment of the scholar, but scarcely to the affection of the people at large. Among the curiosities of literature one comes now and again upon the experiments which those who rush in where angels fear to tread have made, by way of modernizing the Authorized Version, and they do little more than open to us a new and more humiliating conception of the folly of human nature. It perplexes us to understand how so sensible a man as Benjamin Franklin should have made an attempt to paint the lily and gild refined gold; but unfortunately for his fame the attempt itself remains to-day. The man who in early life did not hesitate to compose a new version of the Lord's Prayer was equal in his riper years to paraphrasing Job; and in sober earnest he suggested this as an improvement upon the opening scene of that sublime book: "And it being levee day in heaven, all God's nobility came to court to present themselves before him; and Satan also appeared in the circle as one of the ministry. And God said unto Satan: You have been some time absent; where were you? And Satan answered: I have been at my country-seat and in different places visiting my friends." Not the admirers of Benjamin Franklin, but rather his bitterest foes, might wish that his name should descend to posterity linked to such puerile trifling as this. And meanwhile we say with Robert Browning:

> I prefer, if you please, for my expounder
> Of the laws of the feast, the feast's own founder.

After what has been said as to the influence of the English Bible, we cannot stop with the assurance of its permanence as a standard of good literary form. It endures not for this reason alone or chiefly, but rather because, as no other book does, it brings to us the bread which never perishes, and the water which springs up to everlasting life. In a noble passage which may be quoted in part, because it illustrates his happy use of Scripture, but in the main because it is so supremely true of the Bible, Mr. Ruskin has insisted that literature does its duty "in raising our fancy to the height of what may be noble, honest, and felicitous in actual life, in giving us, though we may ourselves be poor and unknown, the companionship of the wisest spirits of every age and country, and in aiding the communication of clear thoughts and faithful purposes among distant nations, which will at last breathe calm upon the sea of lawless passion, and change into such halcyon days the winter of the world, that the birds of the air may have their nests in peace and the Son of Man where to lay his head."

If such is the province of literature in general, the testimony of full six hundred years proves that it is to an unequalled extent the province of this the greatest masterpiece in our tongue. And who shall venture to measure its influence on the future? As far back as the days of Jerome, a congregation bitterly resented a very slight change in the version of the book of Jonah with which they were familiar, and was only quieted when the old reading had been restored. "They would not tolerate," wrote Augustine to Jerome, "a change in an expression which had been fixed by time in the feelings and memory of all, and had been repeated through so many ages in succession."[1] Our own Bible every year fastens itself more firmly in the love of the whole English speaking family. A Hindu gentleman of fine culture not many years ago drew the attention of his countrymen to the potent influence of the English language in developing the Hindu mind in the present day, and to the intimate connection which existed between that language and the Authorized Version of the English Bible. He held it to be no exaggeration to affirm that its pages had inspired all that was soft and gentle, good and noble about the English nation, "nay,

---
[1] Talbot, pp. 85, 86.

the solid virtues which had helped that great nation," as he said, "in its unexampled advance in civilization and progress had been inspired and strengthened by this great book."[1]

The future of the book is, it would seem, the future of the language. If Shakespeare, and Milton, and Bunyan are to endure as long as our tongue endures, then more confidently still may this be predicted of the Bible. How much such an assertion means it would be hard for us at present to say. Borne upon the crest of this swelling tide, our English Bible will share an earthly immortality to which more largely than any other one work in our language it has itself contributed. Words which were only the extravagance of flattery when spoken of Egypt's dusky queen, are words of truth and soberness when used about this book :

> Age cannot wither it, nor custom stale
> Its infinite variety.

To it alone will ultimately belong the magnificent eulogy of Daniel Webster upon the victorious power, "whose morning drumbeat following the sun, and keeping company with the hours, circles the earth with one continuous and unbroken strain."

---

[1] "Times of India." August 25, 1805.

XI.

IN THE NATION.

"I am interested in the people who made the Bible, but I am more interested in the people whom the Bible makes, for they show me the fibre and genius of Scripture as no mental studiousness, or verbal exegesis can do."—
Dr. C. H. Parkhurst.

CHAPTER XI.

THE BIBLE AND THE NATION.

So perfect is the form in which the message of God has come to us in our English Bible that we are sometimes tempted to speak of that form as though it were in itself of prime importance. We need remember that, while we can no longer separate the truths of Scripture from the language with which for now nearly three centuries they have been associated, yet the authority of the Bible dwells not in the language, but in the truths. As Wordsworth insisted, forms must be the incarnation of thought. The thought of the Scriptures might have been couched in other and inferior language, but it would still have proved itself quick and powerful. In common with other nations, the English and the American people have needed some external law by which to be guided. Without that the Briton would never have risen to an independent existence when the Roman left his shores; and the immigrant landing in this New World might have succumbed before the perils and hardships which, for many years, made his life so trying. The Bible has furnished this external authority, and the true grandeur of these two nations may be traced to the weight which it has from the beginning carried with it.

1. We glance in the first place at the civilizing influence which the Bible has exerted. In his day there was no single man who did so much to humanize the savage lives led by the Northumbrians as Bede, and it is equally true to affirm that no single man is more indissolubly associated than he with the work of teaching the truths of Scriptures and translating them into the vernacular of the people about him. In the ninth century, Alfred impressed himself upon his countrymen, not alone because of his splendid services in war and peace, nor chiefly because of his noble character, but because he was the victorious champion of Christianity against paganism. "Alfred was a Christian hero, and in his Christianity he found the force which bore him through calamity apparently hopeless, to victory and happiness."[1] A life of such tremendous activity as his afforded neither time nor taste for speculative studies. If he learned Latin, it was to popularize its literature with his people. If he translated Boethius, it was to occupy their mind and his own with themes worthy of a nation's most serious thought. If he founded schools, it was with the ambition that free-born English boys should read, with some measure, at least, of ease and accu-

---
[1] "Lectures and Essays," Prof. Goldwin Smith, p. 271.

racy, the Scriptures in their mother tongue. If he collected and gave his sanction to a code of laws, he refused to separate it from the Decalogue. To him chiefly the growth and prosperity of the Saxon people are due, and it must never be forgotten that when the Norman landed at Hastings it was to find a nation in many respects in advance of his own. On the banks of the Seine the Norman left no triumph of architecture superior to the Abbey of Westminster, then fresh from the builders' hands. He brought with him no better priests than those already in possession of the churches, where they read the Scriptures every Sunday in English, and in the same tongue preached their sermons. For a time it was inevitable that civilization should be checked by the Norman conquest. There was little national liberty. There was no royal encouragement given to learning. And it is no more than probable that the translation of the Scriptures into the vernacular, with which we now associate the name of Wycliffe, might have been made three hundred years before he was born if Harold, rather than William, had remained master of the field when the two armies met at Hastings, in that fight which changed the whole future of the English people. It took a long time for the old language to recover its hold; and when, with Norman elements added indeed, it regained the ascendency, England was ready

P

for the Bible of Wycliffe ; and with that came also a new era—an era of purer manners and juster laws.

What happened at that time in the nation at large has often happened in the communities of which it is composed. There is a power in the Bible to civilize which has found frequent illustrations on both sides of the Atlantic. Once let it obtain entrance into any society, and its influence is equivalent to one of those fine acts of which George Eliot says, that they "produce a regenerative shudder through the frame, and make us ready to begin a new life." Methodism in Cornwall, when Wesley preached there, found that county brutal and dissolute ; but substituting for the feeble platitudes of the parish church the word of the Lord, it lifted the population up, and to this hour it is the phraseology of the Bible which is familiar on the lips of the people in the extreme west of England. The same holds in New England, where lives trained up in the teaching of Scripture produced a love of law, a taste for ennobling pursuits, and a sweetness and simplicity of spirit, which made the society in her villages fifty years ago equal to any in Christendom.

2. But the Bible has done more than civilize and refine. It has also proved itself a mighty progressive influence in national life. In the quicken-

ing of that life it has played a great part. No one can say, for example, how the boys and girls, going to school or coming from it, who for seven hundred years have passed before the magnificent west front of Wells Cathedral, have been molded and inspired by its sculptures. The Bible in stone is there. Angels and saints and prophets, scenes from Scripture history, the solemnities of the last judgment, the hope of the resurrection and its despair, must have brought multitudes of men and women into the companionship of biography, history, and theology, and that at a time when books were rare and preaching powerless. The people never lost touch of the truth, and so it is not remarkable that alike, the popular uprisings in favor of liberty and the popular demands for ecclesiastical reform in the fourteenth century, were led by men versed in the Bible. "As sure as God's word is true," said "the good Lord Cobham," in the presence of his king, "the pope is the great antichrist foretold in Holy Writ." For this conviction he was ready to die; and as heretic and traitor, although in truth one of the saints and patriots of those troubled times, he was hung in chains and then burned in London. His manuscript copy of Wy- *Dec. A. D. 1417.* cliffe's Gospels is one of the choicest treasures now preserved in the Baptist College at Bristol. The revolting peasants in the reign of Richard II., marched to the preaching of John Ball, "the mad priest of Kent," from whom, says Green, England "first listened to a declaration of the national equality and rights of men." The rude jingles of ploughmen and mechanics catch their true note from the teachings of Christ. "Jack Miller asketh help to turn his mill aright. He hath grounden small, small: the King's Son of Heaven he shall pay for all." Wycliffe, by his treatises, had stirred the heart of the people. Society, he insisted, was still under the control of God. His "simple priests" had brought the teachings of Scripture and its very words into numbers of country parishes, where "falseness and guile" as the people came to see, "had reigned too long." How powerful and how practical was this preaching of Wycliffe's itinerants, the rhymes of the peasantry testify: "Now right and might, will and skill, God speed every dele"; "Help truth, and truth shall help you." A recent biographer of the poet Chaucer, who himself had little sympathy with the new movement, says with truth: "The connection between Wycliffe's teaching and the peasants' insurrection under Richard II., is as undeniable as that between Luther's doctrines and the great social uprising in Germany, a century and a half afterward."[1] As it circulated among the people, his Bible was a civil almost as much as it

---

[1] A. W. Ward, "Chaucer," p. 16.

Lutterworth Church in 1384
Page 228.

was a religious power. It roused men to struggle for the life that now is as well as for that which is to come. Amid pestilence, famine, and bloodshed the Psalter spoke comfort to innumerable English hearts, and on its words the sorrows and hopes of troubled souls went up to heaven in the dark hours preceding the dawn.

When the day broke at last, the Bible was given due honor. It is supposed that it was first used in national pageantry at the coronation of young Edward VI. "When three swords were brought," writes Strype, the historian, "signs of his being king of three kingdoms, he said there was one wanting. And when the nobles about him asked him what that was, he answered the Bible. 'That book,' added he, 'is the sword of the Spirit, and to be preferred before these swords.' And when the pious young king had said this, he commanded the Bible with the greatest reverence to be brought and carried before him."[1] If this really happened, there was something prophetic in Edward's demand, for as Carlyle says : " The period of the Reformation was a judgment day for Europe, when all the nations were presented with an open Bible, and all the emancipation of heart and intellect which an open Bible involves. England, North Germany, and other powers, accepted the boon, and they have been steadily growing in

---
[1] Westcott, p. 116.

national greatness and moral influence ever since. France rejected it; and in its place has had the gospel of Voltaire, with all the anarchy, misery, and bloodshed of those ceaseless revolutions of which that gospel is the parent."

How powerful was the influence of the Bible in Puritan times we all know. The letters of Cromwell are full of its most passionate words. With the invectives of the Psalms on his lips, the Roundhead rushed on his foe and smote him, as he was often heard to say, as Samson smote the Philistines, *hip and thigh with a great slaughter.* The chapters in "Old Mortality" are no caricatures. They are rather grim, and yet faithful reproductions of scenes and character and conversations familiar in those stormy times in the land of shaggy heath and wild foaming streams. The patriotism of Scotland was nourished in Isaiah, as afterward the hope of the slave in the Southern States was nourished in the Exodus; and in both instances under the Old Testament rather than the New, "despair sublimed to power." The Bible is the book of the nation. Patriotism as much as piety celebrates a victory when on the very spot in London where the Council condemned the remains of Wycliffe to be dug up and burned, the British and Foreign Bible Society builds its central offices.[1] When the Revised Version was

---

[1] The Bible House, Queen Victoria St., London.

ready, its appearance was looked for as eagerly as any event of national importance. The quantity of paper ordered for the edition was so enormous, that had the sheets been piled one upon another in reams as they left the mill, it is said that they would have formed a column ten times the height of St. Paul's Cathedral; or, had they been made into a strip six inches wide, it would have been sufficient "to put a girdle round the world."[1]

There is no other book which can be said to illustrate as does the English Bible the progress of national life. Wycliffe's translation was made at a time when authority was supreme. The people had not found their voice, and only very slowly were they coming to believe that they had any right to a voice at all. Chaucer dared assert in the "Parson's Tale," that "humble folks be Christ's friends," but the parson's brother, the ploughman, is himself a peasant of the subservient type, one of the long and hopeless procession of English laborers who have been taught in the catechism of the national church "to order myself lowly and reverently to all my betters—not to covet nor desire other men's goods; but to learn and labor truly to get mine own living, and to do my duty in that state of life unto which it shall please God to call me." As Richard Jefferies has told us, it was only "after many

---

[1] Geo. W. Moon, "Ecclesiastical English." Preface.

centuries, in the year in which they received the franchise," that the peasants in the parish church were not compelled to sit in a draught. A significant illustration of the way in which the assumption of authority lingered is found in the history of the Revised Version. The heading of Psalm 149, in our modern edition, reads: "The prophet exhorteth to praise God for his love to the church and for that power which he hath given to the church." To this, however, the original edition, 1611, added, "to rule the consciences of man."[1] Lingard, the Roman Catholic historian, is no doubt right in asserting that by his translation of the Bible, Wycliffe put into the hands of his preachers and of the people an engine which must ultimately destroy this condition of civil and religious thralldom. Men were flattered by the appeal to their private judgment; the new doctrines insensibly gained partisans and protectors in the higher classes, who alone were acquainted with the use of letters; a spirit of inquiry was generated, and the seeds were sown of that religious revolution which, in little more than a century, astonished and convulsed the nations of Europe.[2] The authorities were not mistaken in recognizing in the free circulation of the Scriptures, a menace to their monopoly of power; nor are we surprised to

---

[1] Edgar, p. 322.
[2] Lingard's "History of England," Vol. III., p. 311.

find that in many of the dioceses of England—such as Norwich and Lincoln for example—men were punished for reading in the vernacular what was called the "New Law."[1]

When the reign of authority ceased, it was only to give place to that compromise between authority and liberty which men call toleration. There was no broader principle than this recognized when the King James Version appeared, and when the Episcopalian was settling in Virginia, and the Puritan was settling in Massachusetts. But the leaven of the Bible was working; and so, after long centuries the struggle began which only closed in our own day with the complete triumph of religious liberty. How patiently its advances were watched we are reminded by the clamor which was raised when, by a slight misprint, the word "ye" was substituted for "we" in Acts 6 : 3, and the verse was made to read: *Wherefore brethren, look ye out among you, seven men of honest report, full of the Holy Ghost and wisdom, whom ye may appoint over this business.* Here was proof positive of the democratic spirit, and the Scotch Presbyterians were responsible for it. The word of God was to be corrupted in order that it might seem to countenance the people in their claim to elect their own ministers. The General Assembly hastened

---

[1] Angus, p. 40.

to deny the imputation, condemning the error, and declaring that they allowed "no power in the people, but only in the pastors of the church to appoint or ordain church officers." [1]

But the Bible held on its way, and freedom came with it. Twenty-five years before the Continental Congress met in the State House in Philadelphia, the bell was cast whose iron tongue rang out the message which its founders had placed upon it: *Proclaim liberty throughout all the land, to all the inhabitants thereof.* The new liberty bell which celebrates the discovery of America, as well as the Declaration of Independence, bears the old inscription, but around its crown there is the added verse: *Glory to God in the highest, and on earth peace, good will toward men,* while on its face we read the still more significant words: *A new commandment I give unto you, That ye love one another.* Who shall say how wide-spread, or how powerful the influence of the Bible has been in bringing us to our present condition of national equality? The struggle has lasted for hundreds of years. There have been dark and dreadful hours in our history, alike in England and in America, when the Bible has had stern work to do, and has done it. In the first pangs of the anti-slavery conflict, Henry Ward Beecher collected money to furnish to the settlers

---
[1] Edgar, p. 298.

in Kansas both Bibles and rifles. "Some of the rifles were sent in boxes marked 'Bibles,' but without his knowledge, and so passed in safety through Missouri and the enemy's lines. Hence the term 'Beecher's Bibles' came to be applied to these effective weapons."[1] The remedy for the great wrong of slavery was drastic, but it was not hastily applied. Lincoln was more prophet than president, when in language which could only have been written by a constant reader of the Bible, and a reverent admirer of its teachings, he said in his last inaugural :

"Woe unto the world because of offenses, for it must needs be that offenses come, but woe unto that man by whom the offense cometh. If we shall suppose that American slavery is one of those offenses, which in the providence of God must needs come, but which having continued through his appointed time he now wills to remove, and that he gives both to North and South this terrible war as the woe due those by whom the offense came, shall we discern therein any departure from those Divine attributes which the believers in a loving God always ascribe to him? Fondly do we hope, fervently do we pray, that this mighty scourge of war may soon pass away. Yet if God wills that it continue until all the wealth piled by the bondmen's two hundred and

---

[1] Beecher and Scoville's "Life of Henry Ward Beecher," p. 283.

fifty years of unrequited toil shall be sunk and until every drop of blood drawn by the lash shall be paid by another drawn by the sword—as was said three thousand years ago—so still must it be said, the judgments of the Lord are true and righteous altogether."

Where the statesman found his message in the crisis, the poet found his also. So we think of the lad Whittier—he was scarcely more than a lad—as he pictures himself, his day's work over, coming home from the fields, and by the winter fireside having his spirit stirred by the Bible until he drank in the truth to which all his life he was so true, that "men must fear God, and make an end of evil." The progress of the nation is inseparably connected with the honor which it pays to the Bible. A Bible-reading people can never be enslaved. From the bondage in which they may be born they shall surely break away. The line of thought which we have been pursuing cannot better be summed up than in the words of Daniel Webster: "If we abide by the principles taught in the Bible our country will go on prospering and to prosper; but if we and our posterity neglect its instruction and authority, no man can tell how sudden a catastrophe may overwhelm us, and bury all our glory in profound obscurity."

3. The influence of the Bible has been no less marked in the development of liberty where once

it has been gained, than in the struggles inseparable to its acquisition. It is the ally of that eternal vigilance which is the price of freedom. "The sheet anchor of our liberties," as General Grant called it, it is also true that no more powerful agency to promote loyalty exists. Tyndale appealed to Henry VIII. to recognize this when his translation of the Scriptures lay under the royal displeasure. "Is there more danger in the king's subjects than in the subjects of all other princes, which, in every of their tongues have the same, under privilege of their sufferance?"[1] What Coleridge said of the Proverbs holds with equal force of the whole book: "It is the best statesman's manual ever written." When Webster declared that the Christian religion was the foundation of civil society he only echoed the words of Sir Matthew Hale: "Christianity is parcel of the common law," and the roots of that conviction strike deep and far into English history. No one who has studied the annals of the Puritans in New England, no one who has followed the fortunes of the colonists, no one familiar with the spirit of the American Revolution, will be prepared to question the assertion of Secretary Seward that there is a law higher than the Constitution, and regulating the authority of Congress—the law of God and the interests of humanity. This is the

---
[1] Anderson's "English Bible," Vol. I., p. 273.

law which speaks in the Scripture, and Seward is undoubtedly right when he says again that "the existing government of this country could never have had an existence but for the Bible." The speech which first made Lincoln known to the people who were afterward to elect him their president, attracted attention by nothing so much as by its fearless appropriation of one of Christ's own figures. When he was composing it he refused to change it at the earnest solicitation of his supporters. That expression is a truth of all human experience, *a house divided against itself cannot stand.* "The proposition also is true, and has been for six thousand years. I want to use some universally known figure expressed in simple language as universally well-known, that may strike home to the minds of men in order to raise them up to the peril of the times. I would rather be defeated with this expression in the speech, and uphold and discuss it before the people, than be victorious without it."[1]

An influence underlying sound government, the Bible is no less powerful in the development of national spirit. It was patriotism that stimulated the monk Aelfric to translate parts of the Bible into English in the eleventh century. "This book," he says of his version of Joshua, "I turned into English for Ealdorman Ethelward, a book that a prince might study in

A. D. 1023.

---

[1] "Abraham Lincoln." By W. H. Herndon, Vol. II., pp. 66, 67.

times of invasion and turbulence"; and of Judith he writes, as we have already seen: "Englished for your example, that you may also defend your country by force of arms against the outrage of foreign hosts."[1] The bravest hearts of the day beat in unison with the great enterprise of Wycliffe. "One comfort," he says, "is of knights, that they understand much the gospel, and will have to read in English the gospel of Christ's life."[2] It was to national spirit that he appealed, when he claimed for his countrymen the right to have the word of God in their own tongue: "For why are we to be the dregs of the nation?" The passion for adventure and discovery which took the place of knight-errantry has never failed to distinguish the Anglo-Saxon, and the Bible has been his companion in his travels and voyages. The tract which was found among the remains of Sir John Franklin's ill-fated party contained a text of Scripture (Eccl. 12 : 1) underscored; and the highest grave northward on the face of our earth, the grave of another discoverer, bears the cry of David in his penitence, "*Wash me, and I shall be whiter than snow.*"

In rousing the spirit of a people to resist the oppression of its rulers the Bible has done priceless service. From Cromwell, who loved to harangue his troopers from those great texts in the Old Testament which illustrated God's course in history,

---
[1] Talbot, p. 49.   [2] Westcott, p. 20.

to Maurice, who saw, in the same book, "the great witness for liberty, the witness of the sacredness of this earth," we have a long succession of patriotic preachers who have with their stirring words quickened the national pulse. As Prof. George Adam Smith has lately pointed out, the sermons of the Ironsides and Covenanters, as well as their treatises, were inspired by "the narratives of the election of Saul and David, from the part played by the people in the coronation of the latter king, from the subjection of the king to the covenant, as well as from many passages of the prophets. When we remember that the book from which they were drawn was already in the hands and hearts of the common people, we appreciate how much of the liberty which these wonderful centuries secured to us is due to the Old Testament."[1] No better illustration can be found of the close connection between a lofty national spirit and the study of the Bible than is furnished by Scotland. That same Old Testament has for hundreds of years stimulated the patriotism of the country. It has given battle cries to its warriors, and texts to its preachers, and imagery to its orators, and models to its heroes and martyrs, while in humbler and less exciting scenes, "The Cotter's Saturday Night" closes most fitly when,—

---

[1] G. A. Smith, "Preaching of the Old Testament to the Age," pp. 20–22.

> The priest-like father reads the sacred page,
>   How Abram was the friend of God on high;
> Or, Moses bade eternal warfare wage
>   With Amalek's ungracious progeny;
> Or how the royal Bard did groaning lie
>   Beneath the stroke of Heaven's avenging ire;
> Or Job's pathetic plaint and wailing cry;
>   Or rapt Isaiah's wild seraphic fire;
> Or other holy scenes that tune the sacred lyre.

It was on Scottish soil that in our own day Mr. Beecher made one of his noblest pleas for the slave, and the spirit of the Covenanter might have inspired its most solemn words: "Remember! remember! remember! we are carrying out our dead. Our sons, our brothers' sons, our sisters' children, are in this great war of liberty and of principle."[1] The pathos of the allusion gained its power from the fact that the conflict was at that moment waging most fiercely. Others were feeling the same, and turning to the same old book of comfort. At the outbreak of the civil war there was no portion of Scripture so often read by Governor Geo. N. Briggs of Massachusetts as the seventy-seventh Psalm, and in his favorite Bible he has marked completely around with his pencil the fourth verse, *Thou holdest mine eyes waking*.

4. Let us turn from national spirit to national industry. The Bible has constantly upheld the

---

[1] Speech at Glasgow, Oct. 13, 1863.

dignity of labor. The serf found consolation in its pages before his freedom came, the peasant does so amid the monotony of his lot to-day, and so did the Pilgrims in their conflict with hardship on the cheerless New England coast. It ought to be noted that the Bible by discovering new needs opens up fresh avenues for commerce. Civilization and culture, both following in the refining wake of religion, stimulate industries even where they do not actually create them. The copyist in the earlier ages was an artist who commanded high prices for his work; and the printing of the Bible still goes on regardless of the fluctuation of taste and trade. The Royal Exchange in London bears across its portico the words: *The earth is the Lord's, and the fulness thereof;* the electric cable linking the old world to the new flashed a verse of the Bible as its earliest message; and the first parcel sent through the pneumatic postal tube in Philadelphia was a Bible with the label, "The first use of the first pneumatic postal tube in the United States is to send through it a copy of the Holy Scriptures—the greatest message ever given to the world. Covering the Bible is the American flag—the emblem of freedom of sixty-three millions of happy people."

"The best business man I have ever known," Mr. Whitelaw Reid wrote a few years since, "memorized the entire book of Proverbs at twenty-two"; and Prof. G. A. Smith pays a tribute to the service it has rendered to the most successful mercantile nation in the world, when he says: "We cannot overestimate the effect which till a recent date the regular exposition of the book of Proverbs in church and school and home has exercised upon the Scottish character."

5. But there is something even more essential than commerce to a prosperous national life: we mean conduct. And here the influence of the Bible is so generally recognized that it is scarcely necessary for us to dwell upon it at all. Henry VIII. unwittingly owned its power when he complained that the book was "disputed, rhymed, sung, and jangled in every ale-house and tavern." "Of conduct," Matthew Arnold said, "which is more than three-fourths of life, the Bible, whatever people may think or say, is the great inspirer"; and to an earlier generation, Thomas Jefferson bequeathed the conviction that "of all the systems of morality, ancient and modern, which have come under my observation, none appear to me so pure as that of Jesus."

So we come, in closing this chapter, to the cradle of conduct, the home. The Bible is emphatically the book for the home. The royal proclamation on the publi- A.D. 1539. cation of the Great Bible, enjoined upon the king's faithful subjects that "avoiding all contentions and disputations in ale-houses and other places, you use this most high benefit quietly and charitably, every one of you, to the edifying of himself, his wife, and family."[1] The land of the home is the land of the Bible. "For three centuries," Prof. Huxley has said, "this book has been woven into the life of all that is best and noblest in English history; it has become the national epic of Britain, and is as familiar to noble and simple from John O'Groat's house to Land's End, as Dante and Tasso once were to the Italians." Winning its way to the hearts of Royalists and Puritans alike, the Authorized Version held its unique place in English homes—dear to Jeremy Taylor as it was to Richard Baxter, to George Herbert as to John Milton—the one abiding bond of peace when all other bonds were snapped. And in our own time we may remember how in the persistent labors of many years of unrequited and scarcely recognized toil, the scholars of England and America joined in the work of revision. No other literary labor could have united so large a number of accomplished and devoted men. In the majority of cases their passion for the book was undoubtedly first kindled at the firesides of the old and new homes, and the Anglo-American Revision will al-

---
[1] Westcott, p. 105.

ways remain the noblest monument of Christian union and co-operation in this nineteenth century. Who can wonder that in its free circulation among English speaking people, the friends of patriotism and of piety see the true solution of the problems perplexing the minds of civil as well of religious reformers? So Bishop Boyd Carpenter says with truth: "If there is ever to be a communion among the various denominations of Christians throughout the world, it can only come by the honest, patient, careful, reverent, determined, and unself-willed study of the old book of God. Again, if there is ever to be in communities a high and lofty standard of civic duty and individual duty, and of the life which a man and a citizen ought to live among his fellows, then you can only have that by reverencing once more the Bible."[1]

Driven out of her right course a few summers ago, a ship sailing across the Pacific reached an island inhabited by some thirty men and women, who fifteen years before had been shipwrecked upon it. They had failed to save a single relic of their past lives. Clothes and tools and food they had indeed preserved. But the trifling reminders and insignificant mementos of home and fatherland had all perished in the storm which spared to them little more than their own lives. With

---

[1] Speech, 1893.

an agony of longing these lost treasures were remembered. "If," one poor woman cried, "if I had only a rag which I had worn in my old home!" So long as we preserve our English Bible this bitter memory cannot haunt us. It is the sacred center about which cluster and cling all the sweet sanctities of home; and if the home carries in it the nucleus of all government and order, the Bible, which lies at the very heart of the home, is the most powerful influence upon which the patriotism of the nation can rely, and to which the instincts of sound government in the nation may confidently appeal, and from which the prosperity of the nation will in all ages gain its most healthful impulses.

XII.

IN SPIRITUAL LIFE.

"In every heart that is won from the love of sin to the love of God, that is crushed in sorrow and strengthened in the presence of temptation by the writings of psalmists, prophets, and apostles, I find evidence that 'holy men of old spake as they were moved by the Holy Spirit.'"—*R. W. Dale, D. D.*

CHAPTER XII.

THE BIBLE IN SPIRITUAL LIFE.

A PERSONAL friend of Cardinal Manning has told us how, after long and eventful years of absence, duty brought him into the neighborhood of the lovely village in Sussex where he began his career as a minister in the Church of England. As he stood in silence beside the grave of his wife, who had died after a very few years of married life, it must have been difficult to recall the time when this great prince in the Roman Catholic Church had made for himself a happy home in the quiet English parish. His friend, in describing the visit, adds: "I accompanied him into the church and showed him a New Testament with the inscription 'H. E. Manning, 1845.' He laid his hand on the book, saying: 'Times change and men change, but this never changes.'"[1]

So we come to speak of the Bible as the one continuous influence in the inner life of our race. Cardinal Manning was right, "This never changes." Who shall attempt to measure the influence, for example, of the life of Jesus as it is told by the evangelists? Dr. James Hamilton,

---
[1] "Nineteenth Century," 1892, p. 283.

himself one of the saintliest of men, said on one occasion: "I have a great hankering to write the true *Acta Sanctorum*, the story of all the heroic and beautiful deeds which have been impelled by love to the Saviour." Peasants as much as princes for now five hundred years have walked with Jesus along the pages of our English Bible, and their hearts have burned within them as he talked with them by the way, and opened to them the Scriptures. Bidding the philosophers and schoolmen of his times return to the Great Biography, Erasmus said: "If the footprints of Christ are anywhere shown to us, we kneel down and adore. Why do we not rather venerate the living and breathing picture of him in these books? If the vesture of Christ be exhibited, where will we not go to kiss it? Yet were his whole wardrobe exhibited, nothing could represent Christ more vividly and truly than those evangelical writings. Were we to have seen him with our own eyes we should not have so intimate a knowledge as they give of Christ, speaking, healing, dying, rising again, as it were, in our own actual presence."[1]

1. Notice first, the power of the English Bible in kindling life in the soul. When, toward the close of his reign, Henry VIII. tells his subjects that he is "very sorry to know and hear how unreverently that most precious jewel, the word of God, is disputed,

---

[1] Seebohm, "The Oxford Reformers of 1498," p. 257.

rhymed, sung, and jangled in every ale-house and tavern," he unwittingly testifies to this power. Bitter and often purposeless as they have been, the theological conflicts which have so frequently raged in England remind us of it. *Everything lives whither the river cometh.* We hang the weapons of religious controversy in the temple of Scripture as witnesses to the quickening force of the Bible. Listening to the taunts with which polemics darkened the sun and poisoned the air in the English Reformation,— "He is a Pharisee, he is a Gospeller, he is of the new sort, he is of the old faith, he is a new-broached brother, he is a good Catholic father, he is a papist, he is a heretic,"[1]—and mindful of their echoes in our own times, we have at all events this consolation: The Bible wakens the minds of men wherever its voice is heard. In the same reign to which we have just referred, English history furnishes many instances of this power, when the church was either supine or antagonistic. The parishioners of a Somersetshire village cursed with a curate who will not teach them or preach, giving his time rather "to dicing, carding, and bowling," apply to the rector of the next parish, who occasionally comes over and gives them a sermon and teaches them to read the

---

[1] C. Hardwick, "A History of the Christian Church during the Reformation," p. 373.

New Testament. Suddenly, one Good Friday, their own priest enters the pulpit for the first time in many years, and harangues against the new order of things: "If any man will preach the New Testament, if I may hear him, I am ready to fight with him incontinent." "Indeed," the poor people add ruefully, "he applieth in such wise his school of fence so sore continually that he filleth with fear all his parishioners."[1] The annalist of the Reformation, John Strype, has given a vivid picture of the eagerness with which England roused herself to the study of Coverdale's Bible. "Everybody that could, bought or busily read it, or got others to read it to them if they could not themselves; and divers more elderly people learned to read on purpose, and even little boys flocked among the rest to hear portions of the Holy Scriptures read."[2] Before this general passion for the study of the Bible in their mother tongue, the people of England swept aside the affectation of the schoolmen—twenty doctors, as Tyndale put it, expounding one text twenty ways—and went straight to the simple meaning of each verse. Colet, who did more to restore the Bible to its true place than any other English Reformer, sitting alone during the winter vacation, in his chambers at Oxford, was visited by a priest who often attended his expository lectures. They drew

---

[1] Stoughton, p. 146.   [2] Ibid, p. 158.

their chairs to the hearth and began talking. "At length the priest pulled from his bosom a little book, and Colet, amused at the manner of his guest, smilingly quoted the words: *Where your treasure is, there will your heart be also.*" The book turned out to be a copy of the Epistles of Paul which the priest had carefully transcribed with his own hand, and the purpose of his visit was to get light upon the truths of which they were so full. "I ask you now," said he to the great expounder, "as we sit here at our ease, to extract and bring to light from this hidden treasure, which you say is so rich, some of these truths, so that I may gain from this our talk whilst sitting together something to store up in the memory, and at the same time catch some hints as to how, following your example, to seize hold of the main points in the Epistles when I read St. Paul to myself." Colet was only too glad to engage in such congenial work: "My good friend, I will do as you wish. Open your book, and we will see how many and what golden truths we can gather from the first chapter only of the Epistle to the Romans." Only detached rings, as Colet said, carelessly cut from the golden ore of St. Paul as they sat over the winter fire, but showing how much wealth even a single chapter holds![1] No doubt this is only one of a multitude of instances. What all the pageantry of the church

---

Seebohm, "Oxford Reformers," p. 22.

had failed to do, this little volume accomplished. Sharper than the two-edged sword, it pierced the soul and discerned the thoughts and intents of the heart.

Nor were its words easily shaken off. At fifteen years of age a lad heard John Flavel, the Puritan, preach from the text, *If any man love not the Lord Jesus Christ, let him be anathema maranatha.* The sermon seemed to make no impression. A soldier in Cromwell's army and present at the execution of Charles I., the young man cared nothing for religion, and when he emigrated to America lived a whole lifetime in utter neglect of its claims. At length, when one hundred years of age, he was working on his farm at Middlesboro, when suddenly the word to which he had listened eighty-five years before flashed on his mind. He saw once more the preacher rising to pronounce the benediction, he heard his tones as he exclaimed: "How shall I bless the whole assembly, when every person in it who loveth not the Lord Jesus is *anathema maran atha!*" He became bitterly conscious that through all these intervening years no minister had blessed him, and then and there he sought mercy at the hands of a long-neglected Saviour, and to extreme old age, for he lived fifteen years after that time, bore his testimony to the irresistible power of the word of God and to the marvelous mercy of its author.

2. The same divine Spirit who kindles the light keeps it burning. He who by his word quickens life in the soul does not forsake the work of his own hand. We may think, therefore, of the influence of our English Bible in maintaining spiritual life. "The Bible," said Luther, "cannot be understood except through perplexities and temptations." To the times of persecution when the lover of truth and righteousness contested at fearful odds with priests and monarchs who, "red with ravine," shrieked against his creed, we turn for illustrations of Luther's assertion. Could the manuscript copies of Wycliffe's Bible revised by Purvey, tell us their stories, truth might indeed be found to be far more entrancing than fiction. More than a hundred and fifty such manuscripts remain to-day, many of them thumbed and worn with constant use; others much mutilated, torn, and soiled; and some bearing eloquent traces "of the concealment into which they were hurried in times of trouble."[1] When Tyndale's Testament came over to England in consignments from Holland, Thomas Garret, curate of All Hallow's Church, London, was among the first to receive them. We revert to the incident of which we have already made mention. In vain Wolsey searched all London for him. He was followed to Oxford, whither he had carried his treasure. Unsafe there, he fled again,

---

[1] Storrs, "John Wycliffe," p. 69.

but after he had gone a day's journey and a half he was so fearful "that his heart would no other but he must return." Coming back he was immediately apprehended, but again escaped and sought out his friend Dalabor, who has left us the story. Dalabor disguised him in his own coat—"which my mother had given me," and after they had kneeled down both together on their knees, the friends embraced and kissed one the other, . . "and so he departed from me"—the record runs—"apparelled in my coat." The true-hearted friend tells us how when Garret had gone down the stairs from his chamber, and was flying toward Wales, he straightway shut his door, and went into his study; "shutting the second door, and with the New Testament of Erasmus in my hand, kneeled down on my knees, and with many a deep sigh and salt tear, I did with much deliberation read over the tenth chapter of St. Matthew's Gospel, and commit unto God our dearly beloved brother Garret." The prayer was not answered at once in the deliverance of his friend. He was captured, and before many days, in company with Dalabor, and others destined to play an important part in the coming struggle of the Reformation, did penance at the public burning of the obnoxious books.[1]

William Hunter, a London apprentice, who, in the year 1555, was found reading his Bible in the

---

[1] Westcott, pp. 46–49.

chapel of Brentwood, played the man more courageously than did the Oxford scholars. "It was never merry world," cried the priest who discovered him, "since the Bible came abroad in English." Nor could it have added to its joyousness when the brave boy for his alleged heresy was burnt at the stake in his native village. His mother, who plainly shared his views, stood by him to the last. Coming down through the centuries we catch his words still : "In my little pain which I shall suffer, which is but a short braid, Christ hath promised me, mother, a crown of joy ; may you not be glad of that, mother?" The mother knelt down and cried, "I pray God strengthen thee, my son, to the end. Yea, I think thee as well bestowed as any child that I ever bare."[1] At the stake William cast his psalm book into the hands of his brother, Robert; and Robert, who was as courageous as he, said : "William, think on the holy passion of Christ, and be not afraid of death." They seem to have been a family of heroes, nourished in the strong truths of Scripture; for his father, as his son went to be burned, encouraged him to hold out. "God be with thee, son William," and William answered, "God be with you, good father, and be of good comfort ; for I hope we shall meet again, when we shall be merry." At the stake William took a wet, brown faggot and

---

[1] Foxe, Vol. VI., pp. 723-727.

kneeled down thereon and read the fifty-first Psalm."

From a manuscript of John Foxe, the martyrologist, we learn the history of William Maldon. At fifteen years old he would listen to the reading of the Bible by a band of poor men who had all contributed to buy it but his father fetched him away and set him to saying his Latin prayer instead. "This put him upon the thought of learning to read English, that so he might read the New Testament himself; which when he had by diligence effected, he and his father's apprentice bought the New Testament,—joining their earnings together, and to conceal it laid it under the bed-straw, and read it at convenient times." But his mother told her husband of the boy's opinions—how he would not worship the cross which was about him when he was christened, and would be laid on him when he was dead—and the father hastened to his son's chamber, and pulling him out of bed by his hair, whipped him unmercifully. And when the young man bore this beating with a kind of joy, considering it was for Christ's sake, and shed not a tear, the father, more enraged, ran and fetched a halter and put it about his neck, saying he would hang him." The boy escaped, however, and survived to tell Foxe the story, which illustrates the struggles going on in England, no doubt in many a quiet village and country town, between the old order which was doomed to pass away, and the new thought which was destined passing through its baptism of fire, to conquer.[1] The quiet heroism of young apprentices and weak women, as it survives in the records of the dark days of Henry VIII. and Queen Mary, speaks volumes. "You be not ashamed," cried the spy, who had informed against the wife of William Living in the time of Wolsey, "to tell wherefore you come hither!" "No," was the ready answer "that I am not, for it is for Christ's Testament." John Lambert, who was burned in 1538, exclaiming as he lifted his fingers flaming with fire, "None but Christ, none but Christ," was on the side which was destined to prevail when he dared to remonstrate with Henry VIII. in the words of the second Psalm : *Be wise now therefore, O ye kings; be instructed, ye judges of the earth.* The days of the persecution gave place in due time to happier hours, but they left scars in merry England which will never vanish, and lighted, as heroic Hugh Latimer said, such a candle as shall never be put out.

There are worse martyrdoms, however, than those which we have been recalling. In the conflict with doubt and perplexity our Bible has cleared the mind as notably as in the sufferings of the body it calmed and strengthened the spirit.

---
[1] Westcott, p. 107.

Here Chaucer's Poor Parson learned not only how to preach Christ, but also how to live him. Here earnest souls found words for their sighings in early versions of the Psalms, which remain still: "Blessed Lord, have mercy on me, for of myself I have no strength . . . Good Lord, be thou turned unto me, and deliver my soul from this tribulation!"[1] Here the Princess Mary, her body racked with sickness and her heart growing bitter and sour with neglect, found light in her darkness in translating the Gospel of John.[2] Her half-sister Elizabeth has left her testimony to the consolation of Scripture in her copy of Coverdale's New Testament, where one may still read, in her own writing, these words:

> Amonge good thinges
> I prove and finde, the quiet
> life doth muche abounde,
> and sure to the contentid
> Mynde, there is no riches
> may be founde.
>   Your lovinge
>   maistres
>   Elizabeth.

"The writing," says Dore in his description of this little volume which the princess gave to her maid of honor, "is in Elizabeth's fine bold hand."[3]

The first ruler of England who was really worthy to follow Elizabeth in the true succession—

---
[1] Stoughton, p. 68. [2] Ibid., p. 172. [3] Dore, p. 96.

Oliver Cromwell—when himself stricken with fatal illness, heartbroken at the death of his favorite daughter, Mrs. Claypole, listened to Paul's great assurance, *I can do all things through Christ which strengtheneth me*, and put his own hand and seal to it with the words, "This Scripture did once save my life: when my eldest son died, which went as a dagger to my heart; indeed it did." Two psalms—the one hundred and twenty-first and the one hundred and thirty-fifth—were read in the humble home of David Livingstone's father, on the day when the young missionary left it for Africa, and then he and his old father walked from Blantyre to Glasgow, to part with one another on the sailing of the Liverpool steamer; and years afterward the familiar words of the Psalter are woven into the same noble biography when Mrs. Moffat, his mother-in-law, writes to him: "My dear son Livingstone, unceasing prayer is made for you. When I think of you, my heart will go upward: *Keep him as the apple of thine eye. Hold him in the hollow of thine hand*, are the ejaculations of my heart." Indeed, the Psalms have a history of their own of incomparable preciousness; and the pious Scottish worthies, gathering courage and patience from them, would find their hearts beating to music associated with the grandest chapters in their country's annals, as well as with the most inspiring confidences of their spiritual experience. If Cromwell sang the one hundred and seventeenth Psalm with his valorous soldiers on the battlefield of Dunbar, in happier scenes Philip Henry would close with the same words his Sunday morning services, as the fullest expression of a congregation's thanksgiving. We turn to the story of Lazarus with added interest when we see the poet Cowper, walking in the garden, pause before a seat on which some kindly hand has laid a Bible, and open it at this touching chapter, reading until the cloud of horror which has so long hung over him moves away before the record of "so much benevolence and mercy and goodness and sympathy with miserable men." The adjustment of doctrines is not impossible to him who will follow Ruskin's advice: "I never met with but one book in my life that was clear on the subject of works and faith, and that book is the Bible. Read it only on this subject."[1] The clouds of doubt dissipate if with John Duncan we consent to be the passive recipients of truth familiar to us from childhood.[2] The joy which has so often eluded our search and mocked our entreaty is ours when we believe the truth with which William Wilberforce closed his life: "I never knew happiness till I found Christ as a Saviour. Read the Bible; read the Bible."

---

[1] "English Illustrated Magazine," 1893.
[2] "Memoir of Dr. Duncan," by David Brown, p. 155.

For the critical moments of our spiritual history the Bible has a special fitness, but not less is it the book for our daily life. Here, indeed, is the supreme test of its power. As Whittier sings—it is easier—

> To smite with Peter's sword
> Than watch one hour in humble prayer.
> Life's great things, like the Syrian lord,
> Our hearts can do and dare.

To Sir John Simpson, the eminent surgeon, there was no part of Scripture dearer than the twentieth Psalm, and that because he had so often known his mother, in her poverty, sit down and repeat it, and rise refreshed. The children learned to call it "mother's psalm." Nearly half the copies extant of Purvey's version of Wycliffe's Bible are, says Westcott, "of a small size, such as could be made the constant daily companions of their owners." Because of its rarity, the rude block book, printed in the fourteenth century under the name of the "Poor Man's Bible," now fetches a great sum; but the fragments which have survived witness by their torn and soiled condition how much they have been read in humble English homes. Elizabeth's copy of the New Testament bears this record of her days of restraint at Woolwich: "I walk many times into the pleasant fields of Holy Scripture, where I pluck up goodly sentences by pruning, eat them by reading, chew them by musing, and lay them up at length in the high seat of memory; that, having tasted their sweetness, I may the less perceive the bitterness of this miserable life." These words may almost have suggested the passage in which the version of King James is commended to the reader, as "a shower of heavenly bread sufficient for a whole host, be it never so great; and a whole cellar full of oil vessels; whereby all our necessities may be provided for, and our debts discharged." Foxe has the same image in his mind when he says that in the early years of the sixteenth century, "great multitudes tasted and followed the sweetness of God's holy word." And the image changes but not the experience, when the General Assembly congratulates the Scottish people on the day which has dawned at last, "when almaist in every private house the buike of God's law is red and understand in oure vulgarie language."[1] There are sermons in stones to-day for him who deciphers the inscriptions on the old houses in Edinburgh—"He that *tholes* (endures) overcomes"; "O magnify the Lord with me, and let us exalt his name together"; and many like them; and Glasgow preserves the reverence paid in her earlier years to the same book in her municipal motto: "Let Glasgow flourish by the preaching of the word."

The tragedies of life are not all on the battle-

---

[1] Edgar, p. 153.

field, or at the stake. The book which was equal only to the emergencies of our course, but failed in the daily round of trivial tasks, could never have won the place in our hearts which we now accord to the Bible. There is a wealth of meaning which only the simple annals of the people could explain in the phrase, "The Family Bible." That it is the book of the home and the household, is the best proof that it is the book for the heart.

3. Quickened and maintained by the Bible, the spiritual life is nourished from the same source of life even to the last. "Through the only merit of Jesus Christ, my Saviour," Shakespeare commends his soul into the hands of his Creator; and in his confidence in the Advocate before the throne Raleigh takes his pilgrimage. To the sublime strains of the ninetieth Psalm, Hampden's troopers carry him to his last resting-place among the Chiltern hills. The hapless Elizabeth, daughter of Charles I., a captive pining away in Carisbrooke Castle, is found dead one morning, her head upon the Bible, open at the sentence, whose bidding she had gladly obeyed, *Come unto me all ye that labor and are heavy laden, and I will give you rest.* Her brief and broken journey was over. Another pilgrim, worn out in his Master's service, John Bunyan, reaches the end with words which caught their inspiration from that Master's lips: "Take me, for I come to thee." The

gates of the celestial city were opening for him, when McCheyne joyously exclaims: *My soul is escaped as a bird out of the snare of the fowler; the snare is broken, and I am escaped.* The most passionate lover of the country to whom our century has listened, Richard Jefferies, dying in his prime, comes home to his Father, after years of wandering and homelessness, and passes away listening to the word of the Saviour about the decease which he would accomplish at Jerusalem. The greatest of Scottish philosophers, Sir William Hamilton, dies saying: *Thy rod and thy staff, they comfort me;* as, a century or more earlier, he who ranks among the greatest of English apologists—Bishop Butler—had found comfort at the last in the assurance that Jesus Christ was his personal Saviour, because it is written: *Him that cometh to me I will in no wise cast out.* The eminent chemist, Faraday, with the heart of a little child, recalls Paul's famous words, and describes himself as "just waiting"; in the mighty confidence which follows these words, Spurgeon finds his order of release: *I have fought a good fight, I have finished my course, I have kept the faith. Henceforth,* cried Paul, as he lifted his eyes to the glory beyond ; and Whittier may have had the same passage in his mind in his final lines invoking the presence of the one Friend who could bring with him:

> Thy calm assurance of transcendent spheres,
> And the eternal years,

as, without question, had Tennyson when, in words which will live as long as our language, he sang —true lover of the sea which girdles his island home:

> For tho' from out our bourne of Time and Place
> The flood may bear me far,
> I hope to see my Pilot face to face
> When I have crossed the bar.

What has been said in these pages fails of its main purpose if it stops short of the acknowledgment, that it is the spiritual influence of our Bible which makes it as powerful as it is.

Undoubtedly, as Faber asserted, with its uncommon beauty and marvelous English, it lives on the ear as music that can never be forgotten, "so that its felicities often seem to be almost things rather than mere words." But the great literary art of our Bible is not its chief excellence.

Without doubt also, no book equals it in quickening thought. It is supremely the book, which, not thinking for us, makes us think for ourselves; distinguished, Coleridge said, from all other writings pretending to inspiration by the strong and frequent recommendations of knowledge and a spirit of inquiry. But admirable as is its stimulating virtue, not here does its great power lie.

The history of two hemispheres testifies to its

potency in molding the grandest national life. "So great is my veneration for the Bible," John Quincy Adams writes, "that the earlier my children begin to read it the more confident will be my hopes that they will prove useful citizens to their country and respectable members of society." Andrew Jackson spoke words of truth, when in his last illness he declared this book to be "the rock on which our Republic rests." And yet, interwoven though it be with the most heroic chapters in English and American history, this will not account for the hold our Bible has had upon our forefathers on both sides of the sea.

"I utterly dissent," Erasmus made bold to declare, "from those who are unwilling that the sacred Scriptures should be read by the unlearned, translated into their vulgar tongue, as though Christ had taught such subtleties that they can scarcely be understood even by a few theologians, or as though the strength of the Christian religion consisted in men's ignorance." A comparison of the lands where the Bible has freely circulated in the homes of the people with those in which it has been kept in the hands of the priests or locked behind the bars of a foreign tongue, will testify to the wisdom of what Erasmus said, and sustain the statement of Horace Greeley in our own times: "It is impossible to mentally or socially enslave a Bible-reading people." The principles of the Bible are the groundwork of human freedom. But though this book beat in harmony with the passion for liberty which has been so victorious in the history of our race here and in the old world, this does not reveal to us the richest source of its wealth.

Giving to the judgment of Coleridge already quoted, that "intense study of the Bible will keep any writer from being vulgar in point of style," a much broader significance than he intended, we may praise the Bible for its sway over our intellectual and moral aspirations. With John Stuart Mill we may believe that "the Bible and Shakespeare have done more than any other books for the English language, introducing into the soul of it such grand ideas expressed with such sublime simplicity." Even yet, however, we are left without the key to its incomparable power. No doubt the Bible merits Ruskin's eulogium as "the guide of all the arts and acts of the world which have been noble, fortunate, and happy"; and multitudes of men and women are grateful that their experience has corresponded with that of Professor Stuart Blackie, when he says that his life has been cleansed and elevated, because—to use his own words: "I was not more than fifteen years old when I was moved to adopt the ideal ethics of the gospel as my test of sentiment and my standard of conduct; and to this I adhered steadily thenceforward, just as a young seaman would stick to his compass and to his chart, and a young pedestrian to his map of an unknown country." But incalculable as is the moral potency of the Bible, not even this constitutes its loftiest claim to our reverence.

We strike a chord even deeper when we speak of this book as the balm for so many of the ills to which our flesh is heir, the heart's-ease of innumerable lives in every generation. "I am asked," Mr. Gladstone writes, "what is the remedy for the deeper sorrows of the human heart—what a man should chiefly look to in his progress through life as the power that is to sustain him under trials, and enable him manfully to confront his afflictions. I must point to something which, in a well-known hymn is called, 'The old, old story,' told in an old, old book, and taught with an old, old teaching, which is the greatest and best gift ever given to mankind." Such words as these bring us within sight of the citadel; but yet even they leave us still outside its walls.

The secret of the Bible, its peculiar secret, is its supernatural grace. The Spirit breathes from its pages. We may have no human theory of inspiration, but was not Coleridge right when he said that "the Bible without the Spirit is a sun dial by moonlight?" In her rich, deep voice, George Eliot, as her life drew to its close, would read daily from this book "a very precious and sacred book to her, not only from early associations, but also from the profound conviction of its importance in the development of the religious life of man." To the end it will be true, as John Robinson said to the Pilgrim Fathers when they embarked on the Mayflower, that "the Lord has more truth yet to break forth out of his holy word." After preaching the gospel for forty years, Spurgeon hands in his testimony: "I have only touched the hem of the garment of divine truth, but what virtue has flowed out of it. The word is like its Author—infinite, immeasurable, without end." It is what no other book is, the authoritative voice to the soul. "I see," said the historian Hallam, "that the Bible fits into every fold and crevice of the human heart. I am a man, and I believe that this is God's book because it is man's book." As Coleridge exclaimed, "This book finds me." Is not this our evidence of its divine origin? To listen to it is to have the spirit of questioning disarmed by "the expulsive power of a new affection." Dr. Dale's experience is ours: "I think that the universal experience of devout Christians will sustain me when I say that in reading the New Testament the idea of the authority of the book, as a book, is hardly ever thought of. The book, explain it how we may, vanishes. The truth I read there shines in its own light. . . Whether the writers of the New Testament are infallible or not, is a question which rarely occurs to me. Somehow, when they tell me a truth, I come to know it for myself : this truth is mine and not merely theirs. Practically, the Bible does not come between me and God."[1] This self-evidencing power the Bible offers to the humblest as well as to the profoundest of its readers. The poor woman in Cowper's poem stands in clearer light than does Voltaire, although she

> Just knows, and knows no more, her Bible true;
> A truth the brilliant Frenchman never knew.

Perhaps we have failed to appreciate at its full value the power of the inner life in the men who were foremost in giving us our English Bible. Tyndale was in solemn earnest when he closed his preface with Paul's request, " Pray for us " ; and Purvey had not associated with Wycliffe in vain when he wrote of the qualifications for the true interpreter of Scripture : " He hath need to live a clean life and be full devout in prayers, and have not his wit occupied about worldly things ; that the Holy Spirit, author of wisdom and knowledge and truth, dress him in his work, and suffer him not for to err. By this manner . . . men may come to true and clear translating and true understanding of Holy Writ, seem it never so hard at the beginning."[2] To this spirit of self-

---

[1] " Protestantism; Its Ultimate Principles," pp. 50, 51.
[2] Westcott, p. 21.

surrender on the part of Wycliffe and Tyndale, and others who followed their lead, is it due that the Bible is so well able in our noble version to explain itself. The wish of the old writer has been gratified, when he desired that the Scriptures might be "so purely and pliantly translated that it needed neither note, gloss, nor scholia; so that the reader might once swim without a corke."[1] John Brown, of Harper's Ferry, wrote these true words in his prison Bible: "There is no commentary in the world so good in order to a right understanding of this blessed book, as an honest, childlike, and teachable spirit."

We live in the day when, as never before, our English Bible circulates throughout the world. But let us remember that the multiplication of Bibles means the multiplication of witnesses rising to testify for us or against us. How pathetic the words which poor Hartley Coleridge wrote in his Bible, as from his twenty-fifth birthday he reviewed a wasted life,

> When I received this volume small
>   My years were barely seventeen
> When it was hoped I should be all
>   Which once, alas, I might have been.
>
> And now my years are twenty-five,
>   And every mother hopes her lamb,
> And every happy child alive,
>   May never be what now I am.

---

[1] Edgar, p. 150.

We are reminded of another boy of high promise, a young Scottish poet who died on the threshold of life, with the prophecy of his boyhood all unfulfilled, and his Bible on his pillow, with these last lines penned by his feeble hand :

> 'Tis very vain for me to boast
> How small a price my Bible cost;
> The day of judgment will make clear
> 'Twas very cheap—or very dear.

In no better way can we close our study of the history and influence of the English Bible than with the comment of the man who more perhaps than any other, flung open the doors of this great treasure-house in the days of the Protestant Reformation. Erasmus pictures the true spirit in which the word of God must be studied when he says of the student coming to its pages : " Let him approach, not with an unholy curiosity, but with reverence ; bearing in mind that his first and only aim and object should be that he may catch and be changed into the spirit of what he there learns. It is the food of the soul ; and to be of use must not rest only in the memory, but must permeate the very depths of the heart and mind."

LITERATURE.

The literature of the subject is very extensive. The writer desires to express his special obligation to the following books:

BRIEF NOTES ON THE CRITICAL HISTORY OF THE TEXT AND ENGLISH VERSIONS OF HOLY SCRIPTURE. By Joseph Angus, M. A., D. D. London.

THE ANNALS OF THE ENGLISH BIBLE. By Christopher Anderson. First edition. London, 1845.

"ENGLISH BIBLE." ENCYCLOPÆDIA BRITANNICA. By the Rev. J. H. Blunt, M. A.

OLD BIBLES: AN ACCOUNT OF THE EARLY VERSIONS OF THE ENGLISH BIBLE. By J. R. Dore. London, 1888.

THE ENGLISH BIBLE. By John Eadie, D. D., LL. D. 2 Vols. London, 1876.

THE BIBLES OF ENGLAND. By Andrew Edgar, D. D. London, 1889.

A HANDBOOK OF THE ENGLISH VERSIONS OF THE BIBLE. By J. I. Mombert, D. D. London, 1888.

COMPANION TO THE REVISED VERSION OF THE NEW TESTAMENT. By Alex. Roberts, D. D. New York, 1881.

A COMPANION TO THE GREEK TESTAMENT AND THE ENGLISH VERSION. By Philip Schaff, D. D. New York, 1883.

A SUPPLEMENT TO THE AUTHORIZED ENGLISH VERSION OF THE NEW TESTAMENT. By the Rev. F. H. Scrivener, M. A. London, 1843.

OUR ENGLISH BIBLE: ITS TRANSLATIONS AND TRANSLATORS. By John Stoughton, D. D. London.

A GENERAL VIEW OF THE HISTORY OF THE ENGLISH BIBLE. By Brooke Foss Westcott, B. D. London, 1868.

INDEX.

Adams, John Quincy: on the Bible 268
Addison, Joseph: "The spacious firmament," etc. 196
Aelfric, Abbot: translations from the Old Testament............ 14, 238
Aidan, Bp., and Lindisfarne.. 4
Aldhelm's Psalter............ 11
Aldred: his Anglo-Saxon gloss of the Gospels...... 14
Alfred the Great.......... 13, 224
American Bible Union........ 157
Anderson, Christopher: Annals of the Bible......*Preface*
Arnold, Matt.: on the Bible and Conduct............ 243
Art and the Bible............ 201
Authorized Version..... 93 *et seq.*
   revisers of 98, 102
   instructions to............. 102
   published 105
   its reception.............. 106
   growing popularity of...... 107
   its style and sources of its strength.. 140, 141, 182, 183

Ball, John: the mad priest of Kent 228
Bede: work of.................. 12
   his death 13
Beecher, H. W........... 234, 241
Bible, The: the basis of Christian union........... 245
   Bishops' Bible, the..... 77 *et seq.*
   English of............ 139, 140
   character of .... 181 *et seq.*
   first completion in English 55
   and conduct.................. 243
   the "Great"......... 55 *et seq.*
   and national industry...... 241
   influence of on the language .... 174 *et seq.*
   in English literature, 171 *et seq.*
                        185 *et seq.*
   in the nation......... 223 *et seq.*
   origin of the title........... 18
   in spiritual life...... 249 *et seq.*
Briggs, Governor: quoted... 241
Bright, John............. 202, 205
Bristol College, England: copy of Tyndale's Testament in.................. 39

INDEX.

Broughton, Hugh: translates parts of the Old Testament.................... 89
Bryant: "Thanatopsis"...... 197
Bunyan, John: forms his style on the Bible........ 206
Burke, Edmund: quoted... 201
Byron: indebted to the Bible 197

Caedmon, versified histories 12
Carlyle, Thomas: on *Job*... 204
Caxton, William: his printing press in Westminster 9
Chaucer: his use of Scripture............... 16, 178, 231
Chillingworth, W., and "The Religion of Protestants" 215
Civilizing influence of the Bible................ 224 *et seq.*
Clough, A. H.: quoted...... 214
Cobham, Lord, and his copy of Wycliffe's Gospels.... 227
Colet, Dean: conversation of with a priest............ 252
Constantinople: fall of........ 207
Coverdale, Miles: birthplace of 55
  training of 56
  work of as translator........ 57
  his first Bible............... 57–60
  reception of first Bible of.. 61
  leaves England............... 71
  return and old age of...... 73
  character and work of.. 73, 74
  peculiarities of his version.. 135

Coverdale, Miles: the eagerness of the people to read his Bible............ 252
Cowper, William......... 196, 262
Cranmer, Archbishop,...... 16, 57
  [and Coverdale]...... 60, 64
Cromwell, Oliver: his appreciation of the Bible...... 260
Cromwell, Thomas: favors Bible translation 56
  57, 60, 64, 66
  his fall........................ 67

Dickens, Charles: on the style of the New Testament......................... 191
  his respect for Scripture... 192
Douay Old Testament........ 89

Edward VI.: favorable to Bible revision............ 69
  the Bible at his coronation 229
Elizabeth, Queen: her policy 77
  her copy of the New Testament.................. 260, 263
Ellicott, Bp.: on the need for revision......... 147, 148
  promotes American co-operation 152
English of the versions 131 *et seq.*
Erasmus: impulse given by to the study of the New Testament 47, 208
  reverence of for the New Testament..... 250, 268, 274

INDEX. 279

	PAGE
Everett, Edward: on the *Proverbs*	203
Flavel's text remembered	254
Franklin, Sir John, and his Arctic explorers	239
Franklin, Benjamin: quoting *Habakkuk*	205
his paraphrase of *Job*	217
Froude, J. A.: eulogy of Tyndale	182
Garret: labors and sufferings of	41, 255
Geneva: the home of the Protestant exiles	71
Genevan Testament	72
Bible, *ibid.*: its popularity	80
described	136–139
Great Bible, The	66–68, 213
Gildas: quoted	10
Gladstone, Hon. W. E.: on the Bible	270
Gospels: early versions of	13
Handel: on the "Messiah"	213
Henry VIII.: in relation to the Great Bible	67
subsequent opposition to the English Bible	68
Hereford, Nicholas de: disciple of Wycliffe	23
his work as a translator	23, 24
Home, the, and the Bible	243
Hunt, Holman: on "The Light of the World"	210

	PAGE
Hunter, William: martyrdom of	256
Huss, John: testimony of to Wycliffe	29
Huxley, Professor: on the Bible and English life	244
Irving, Washington: stimulated by the Bible	212
Jackson, Andrew: on the Bible	268
Jerusalem Chamber, the,	150, 167
Johnson, Dr. Samuel: on *Ruth*	205
Joye [or Roye]: Tyndale's amanuensis	37
reprints Tyndale's New Testament	43
Tyndale's feud with him	49–51
Latimer, Hugh: sets up the Great Bible in Worcester monastery	68
Liberty Bell, the	234
Lindisfarne Abbey	11
Lingard: on the influence of Wycliffe's Bible	23
Livingstone, David, and *the Psalms*	261
Maldon, William: martyrdom of	258
Manning, Cardinal: on the unchanging Bible	249

INDEX.

Manuscripts, Early........ 9 *et seq.*
Manuscripts of Wycliffe's Bible still extant......... 255
Mary, Queen: translating Gospel by John........... 260
   prohibits the reading of the Scriptures.............. 70
Matthew, Thos.: his Bible.. 63
   mystery about him.......... 63
Miller, Hugh: on the story of Joseph.................. 211
Milton, John: hymn of........ 196
   on the Bible................... 201
More, Sir Thomas: opposes Tyndale's translation of the New Testament..... 40
   a patron of Coverdale...... 60

Nix, Bishop: favors destruction of Tyndale's Testament...................... 42
Newman, Cardinal: on Bible translation 183
Norman Conquest: its influence on scholarship 15, 225

Parker, Archbishop.......81 *et seq.*
Poetry, English, and the Bible................. 196 *et seq.*
Printers' Errors............ 142–144
Puritans: love of for the Bible...................... 230
Purvey, John: Bible translator 24

Purvey, John: his principles of translation............24, 25
   his character................... 25

Raleigh, Sir W.: quoted..203, 214
Rogers, John.............62 *et seq.*
Revision: recommended in 1645 111
   why?....................112 *et seq.*
Revised Version, the: resolution looking to......... 147
   a Committee of Revision formed 149
   American scholars co-operate.................... 152 *et seq.*
   time given to the work..... 151 *et seq.*
   division of labor............. 156
   need of a Revision......... 157
   changes found in R. V..... 158
   New Testament published, 159
   entire Bible published...... 160
   Dean Burgon's attack on... 162
   other criticisms of......162–164
   the English of the Revision............................ 166
   eagerness to read............ 230
Rheims New Testament 88
Rushworth: version of the Gospels..................... 13
Ruskin, John: quoted 199, 204, 218, 262

Science and the Bible........ 209
Scott, Sir W.: his familiarity with the Bible..... 190 *et seq.*

Shakespeare : his use of the Bible............ 185 *et seq.*
Smith, Prof. Geo. A. : on *Proverbs* 243
Smith, Dr. Miles : " Address to the Reader," in the Authorized Version...... 104
South, Robert : quoted........ 200
Spenser, Edmund.............. 212
Stanley, Henry M. : experience of with the Bible... 200

Taverner, Richard : his Bible 65
Tennyson : indebted to the Bible........197 *et seq.*, 267
Thackeray, W. M. : use of the Bible........... 194 *et seq.*
Toleration : era of............ 233
Tomson, Lawrence : translation of New Testament.. 89
Tunstall, Bishop............. 40, 67
Tyndale, William : his life of.................... 33 *et seq.*
aspires to give the Bible in English to the people... 34
issues two editions of the New Testament.......... 38
publishes the Pentateuch.. 43
revision of the New Testament...................... 43
imprisonment and death of......................... 44, 45
his character................ 45
superiority of his work..... 47

Tyndale, William : the English of his version...134, 184
influence on our language.. 180
his version and the authorized..................... 181
Ulfilas translating the Scriptures into Gothic......... 175

Webster, Daniel : a student of the Bible............ 201
Wells Cathedral : west front.. 227
Whittier and the Bible........ 236, 263, 266
Wilberforce, Bishop : resolution of in convocation... 147
Wolsey, Cardinal : persecuting Garrett............ 41
also Barnes..................... 56
Wordsworth, William : ode of to immortality............ 197
Wycliffe, John : life of...21 *et seq.*
translation of Apocalypse and Gospels by............ 22
entire New Testament..... 22
Old Testament............... 23
assisted by Hereford........ 23
his death..................... 24
traces of ecclesiastical influence in his version... 26
its beauty.................... 26
spread of his influence... 27-29, 178
manuscripts of his Bible still extant............ 255

www.ingramcontent.com/pod-product-compliance
Lightning Source LLC
Chambersburg PA
CBHW032053220426
43664CB00008B/985